Tom Quick

DARTMOOR INNS

Tom Quick

DARTMOOR INNS

History and Stories of all the Inns
and Public Houses
within the Dartmoor National Park

DEVON BOOKS

First published in Great Britain in 1992 by Devon Books

ⓒ Tom Quick, 1992

British Library Cataloguing in Publication Data. A catalogue record for this book is available
from the British Library.

ISBN O 86114 880 0

ACKNOWLEDGEMENTS

This book would not have been possible without the help of Tony Marriott,
who read the proofs, Lesley White, who typed the original material, John
Stone (the Dartmoor Snapper) who developed about 100 yards of black and
white film, and Paul Bowden who acted as courier in collecting and
delivering the photographs.
Thanks are also due to Jack Billings, Carol Comer, Nicholas Fry, David
German, Lesley Jerrett, Wilf Joint, Chris Jones, Sally Jones, Idris Kerswell,
Graham Lock, Wendy Major, Jack Reddaway, John Sergeant, Dick Wills
and to all the landlords and landladies, past and present, for their assistance,
and for their permission to reproduce the old photographs used in this book.
Thanks also to David German for the photograph of the Royal Oak,
Meavy; to Elizabeth Stanbrook for the photo of Haytor Vale; and to the
Devon Record Office for the photo of John Swete's watercolour of the
Saracen's Head (ref. 564M/16p.141). Also thanks are due to the staff at the
West Country Studies Library, Exeter.

DEVON BOOKS
Official Publisher to Devon County Council
Unit 1 Chinon Court
Lower Moor Way,
TIVERTON EX16 6SS
(Tel: 0884 243242)
(Fax: 0884 243325)

and

397 Topsham Road
EXETER EX2 6HD

Printed and bound by BPCC Wheatons Ltd, Exeter

INTRODUCTION

The aim of this book is to provide the history and stories connected with the inns that lie within the Dartmoor National Park. It is not intended to be a 'Good Pub Guide'; I leave you to decide for yourself whether or not the food, drink and accommodation that they provide come up to your own standards. When you visit these inns, try to really enjoy their history, meet the characters amongst the locals that frequent them, and get to know them as I have done.

Many of the older generation who could relate historical facts and anecdotes are no longer with us, but fortunately some of those stories have been passed down to us before being lost forever. During my research for this book I have been honoured to meet many of those interesting people. Different doors have been opened to me and I have heard many stories, most factual, many amusing, and some that I dare not put into print, but all of them tell us of the origins of the inns and the life and times that have evolved in and around them. Some of the pubs have not had as colourful a history as others, but they have all been included, from the small 'local' to the larger better known inns.

Tom Quick
Exeter 1992

To my daughter Jacquelyn Louise

PUBLISHER'S NOTE

Although the terms Public House, and Inn have specific meaning within the law, they have become interchangeable through modern usage and are used as such throughout this work. All information relating to specific establishments is correct, as far as is known, at the time of going to press.

Two of the Inns included, the Highwayman's and the Welcome Stranger, are sited just outside the National Park Boundary.

INDEX

	Name	Page		Name	Page
1	Anchor Inn	1	44	Packhorse Hotel	75
2	Anglers Rest	2	45	Palk Arms	76
3	Artichoke Inn	3	46	Peter Tavy Inn	78
4	Bay Horse	5	47	Plume of Feathers	80
5	Bearslake Inn	6	48	Plymouth Inn	82
6	Bell Inn	8	49	Post Inn	83
7	Bridford Inn	10	50	Prewley Moor Arms	84
8	Bullers Arms	11	51	Prince of Wales	86
9	Burrator Inn	12	52	Red Lion	88
10	Carpenters Arms	15	53	Ring 'O' Bells - Chagford	89
11	Castle Inn	17	54	Ring of Bells - North Bovey	92
12	Church House Inn	20	55	Rising Sun	94
13	Cleave, The	22	56	Rock Inn - Haytor Vale	96
14	Cornwood Inn	24	57	Rock Inn - Yelverton	97
15	Dartmoor Inn - Lydford	25	58	Royal Standard	99
16	Dartmoor Inn - Merrivale	28	59	Royal Oak - Ashburton	102
17	Devil's Elbow	32	60	Royal Oak - Dunsford	103
18	Devon Tors	33	61	Royal Oak - Meavy	105
19	Drewe Arms	35	62	Royal Oak - South Brent	107
20	East Dart Hotel	37	63	Rugglestone Inn	109
21	Elephant's Nest	39	64	Sandypark Inn	110
22	Exeter Inn	40	65	Seven Stars	112
23	Fleece & Firkin	43	66	Skylark Inn	113
24	Forest Inn	45	67	Sun Inn	115
25	Fox & Hounds	47	68	Tavistock Inn	116
26	George Inn	49	69	Teignhouse Inn	119
27	Globe Inn - Buckfastleigh	51	70	Three Crowns Hotel	120
28	Globe Inn - Chagford	52	71	Tors Inn	122
29	Golden Lion	54	72	Tradesmans Arms	124
30	Highwaymans Inn	55	73	Two Bridges Hotel	125
31	Kestor Inn	58	74	Union Inn	128
32	Kings Arms - Buckfastleigh	59	75	Victoria Inn	130
33	Kings Arms - South Zeal	60	76	Walkhampton Inn	131
34	Lantern Inn	62	77	Warren House Inn	133
35	Leaping Salmon	63	78	Watermans Arms	135
36	Leg 'O' Mutton	64	79	Welcome Stranger	136
37	London Inn - Ashburton	65	80	White Hart Hotel	137
38	London Inn - Horrabridge	67	81	White Horse Inn	139
39	London Inn - South Brent	68	82	White Thorn Inn	141
40	Mary Tavy Inn	69			
41	Northmore Arms	70			
42	Old Inn	71			
43	Oxenham Arms	73			

1: Anchor Inn

Station Road, South Brent
Tel: South Brent (0364) 73135

The date when the Anchor Inn was first built is uncertain, but records show that it was in existence in 1850 when Mr Arthur Langworth was the innkeeper. The name of the inn is said to be connected with men that were 'conscripted' here by Royal Navy press gangs. It is reputed that there are tunnels running from beneath the building and if patrons had warning of any approaching press gangs they would hide in them until it was safe to leave.

In 1990 the Inn was almost completely destroyed by fire and has since been totally rebuilt, still retaining much of its original character.

2: Anglers Rest

Fingle Bridge, 1 mile from Drewsteignton.
Tel: Drewsteignton (0647) 21287

The Anglers Rest was built in 1957 and was first licensed in the same year. The spacious 'Poachers Bar' has been furnished in traditional Dartmoor style, complete with an oak-beamed ceiling and large stone fireplace.

There has been a refreshment establishment on this site for nearly a hundred years. Before that, visitors to Fingle Glen would have used the thatched 'Old Mill', which was situated 300 yards further downstream on the opposite side. This building was unfortunately destroyed by fire in 1894.

It was in 1897 that Mrs Jessie Ashplant first started selling teas here following a suggestion by the Rector of Drewsteignton, Rev. Richard Peek, that something was needed to replace the Old Mill. For 10 years she traded in the open air before her tea shelter was opened in 1907.

3: Artichoke Inn

In the village of Christow, 1 mile from the B3193.
Tel: Christow (0647) 52387

The exact date when the Artichoke Inn was first built is uncertain but it is thought that it could date back to the 14th century. During the 19th and early 20th century Christow was a bustling village with the mines and quarries nearby employing many workers. The Teign Valley Railway was also a source of employment. The village at that time supported two inns, The Palk Arms and the Artichoke Inn. With the closure of the above industries, trade dwindled and the Palk Arms closed down.

Originally there were two cottages adjoining The Artichoke Inn, which has since expanded with the acquisition of the cottage nearest to it, in 1970. This was then converted into the dining room. The remainder of the interior consists of a split-level public bar which has a low ceiling, bench seats, and the lower half of the walls wood panelled. There is also a large stone

fireplace. On the wall next to the rear door and placed in a glass case is an interesting dart board. It is smaller than normal, it has no trebles on it and the numbers are not in the usual order. This board was found in 1984 in a stream nearby. The wall separating the public bar from the lounge bar was removed in 1962 thus forming the through bar seen today.

Over the years there has been more than one larger-than-life character associated with this inn. In the early 1930s there was 'Butcher' Davis, who with his white curly hair and cigarette hanging from his lips, looked an imposing sight. As well as being the landlord he used to do some butchering as a sideline. On Boxing Day each year he would provide all his regular customers with a free Christmas meal. In the 1950s there were three regulars who, in the evenings would entertain the other customers at the inn. Jimmy Norman played the fiddle and was known as Jimmy the Fiddler, Bill Barker played the tin whistle (sometimes by his nose), and finally there was Harry Stonelake who would tap dance to the music provided by his companions. Then in the 1960s Henry Edwards, a local farmer, would ride his cart-horse to the inn, knock on the side door, order his pint of ale and proceed to drink it while still sitting on his horse. While this was going on his horse would have its head in through the doorway and its rear end stuck out into the middle of the narrow road!

4: Bay Horse

In North Street, Ashburton.
Tel: Ashburton (0364) 52838

The Bay Horse Inn is thought to have been built in the 17th century although it is not certain how long it has been an inn. Originally it was called the Barnstaple Inn. There used to be only one large room upstairs where many a traveller laid their bed roll on the floor to spend the night. The original name of the inn came from the time when it was just a cider house and fishermen from Brixham would stay the night here before carrying on to Barnstaple. The route along the 'Mariner's Way' was much frequented by fishermen moving between the ports on the North and South

Devon coasts in search of work.

From October 1928 Mabel Short and her husband Ernest ran the inn. Sadly her husband died in 1953 and from then on, until 1974 when she was 75 years old, she continued on her own to look after the inn. During this time she acquired quite a reputation for keeping a clean, trouble-free inn. She was frequently known to send some of her customers home early if they were drinking a little bit too much, saying to them 'Go on home now I'd hate to think that you might have an accident due to too much drink', or 'Don't you think it's about time you went home to the Sunday lunch that your good wife has cooked for you?' Woe betide anyone trying to cause trouble in Mabel's inn.

The original thatched roof has been replaced by slate and, in 1970, the interior walls separating the smaller public bar and lounge bar were removed thus forming the large main bar seen today. This room has a low beamed ceiling, subdued wall lights and large stone fireplace. The games room, once a beer cellar, was altered in 1988. When the plaster on the walls

was removed two small windows that are thought to be at least 300 years old were discovered.

The inn is said to be haunted by the spirit of a young girl who died during the last century from diptheria; she has been heard sobbing in one of the rooms upstairs. There has also been the sound of children running along the corridor upstairs.

5: Bearslake Inn

On the A386 Okehampton-Tavistock road, below the village of Sourton.

Tel: Bridestowe (083 786) 334

The Bearslake Inn is made up of many buildings thought to date from the 13th century, although it has only been an inn for the past ten years. The main part is a beautifully restored Dartmoor longhouse, complete with thatched roof. For many years and up to the early 1960s these buildings were part of a working farm, with Mr Jury being the tenant farmer. Today's commercial kitchen was the dairy, the snug bar used to be a cart shed and the cottage adjoining the inn was the pigsty. The farm was part of the Leawood Estate, owned by Lt-Colonel Calmady Hamlyn. During the 1960s the farm was used only to house the animals, fell into a state of decay, and was subjected to a demolition order.

It was at this time that the lower half of the buildings (from the hedge downwards) was leased out to Mr Sweet, a gentleman who was a Lancia car fanatic. Along with his wife, he started up a business selling cream teas. His collection of cars would often attract passers-by to his property.

In 1970 the property was bought by Geoff and Roz Leigh-Ford and they turned it into a restaurant, and a little later on into a wine bar. They later sold out to a Scots lady named Morag, who built up quite a reputation for her marvellous cream teas. However due to the lack of accommodation for guests she in turn moved on, selling out to Mike and Bridget Power. Shortly after, they were able to buy the other half of the buildings, which had now been derelict for some fifteen years (having reverted back to the Leawood Estate). They then applied for, and were granted, a licence to sell alcohol, and they opened up the Bearslake Inn. The present landlord Ray and his wife Thelma took over the inn three years ago.

If you stay the night at the inn and hear the sound of a young girl crying, you will not be the first. Ray and several other guests in the past have also heard these sounds. The crying has been traced to room 2, but upon opening the door, there has been no one to be seen and the crying has stopped. Maybe this is the ghost of the little girl who had a riding accident and had been confined to bed during her convalescence. She one day ventured from her sick bed and while walking down stairs, tripped and fell. She later died of her further injuries.

6: Bell Inn

In the centre of Moretonhampstead, 14 miles from Exeter.
Tel: Moretonhampstead (0647) 40437

The date when the Bell Inn was first built is uncertain although it is thought to be made up from cottages dating from the 16th century. There have been suggestions that it may at one time have been used as a church, but of this there is no evidence. The first mention of it being an inn is in 1799; one year later it was sold for £440. During 1845 the building was almost completely destroyed by one of the many fires which have ravaged Moretonhampstead over the years.

The inn consists of the Haytor bar and the Colwell bar and, supporting the ceiling between these two rooms, is an interestingly carved oak beam.

Its origin is unknown but it is reputed to date from the 13th century; there used to be a carving of a king's head in the centre of it, but unfortunately this was destroyed sometime in the past.

During the 19th century, the inn was a meeting place for wrestling matches, but now the only meetings taking place here are of a more friendly nature; the British Legion, the Royal Antediluvian Order of Buffaloes, and the Thatchers' Association hold their gatherings upstairs. There is rumoured to be a ghost residing here, however it seems that anything which happens and cannot be explained gets blamed on Jim Letts. Jim was a former landlord who owned the inn for nineteen years. If a door suddenly blows open or a picture falls from the wall someone will say 'Jim Letts did that'.

7: Bridford Inn

In the centre of Bridford, 7 miles from Exeter.
Tel: Christow (0647) 52436

The Bridford Inn was converted into an inn during the mid 1960s from two 17th century cottages, still retaining some of the original stone walls and fireplaces. The main oak posts that support the wooden-beamed ceiling, came from oak left over during the construction, at the Appledore boatyard, of the replica of the Pilgrim Fathers' ship, *The Mayflower*. The wood used in the making of the wide bar top came from Boots the chemist's in Exeter when they modernised one of their shops. The inn has taken over the licence and replaced the 'Old Harriers' (now a private residence) as the only inn in Bridford.

8: Bullers Arms

Mill Street, Chagford, 5 miles from Whiddon Down
& 2.5 miles from Moretonhampstead. Tel: Chagford (0647) 432348

The date when the Bullers Arms was built is uncertain although parts of it
are thought to date from the 16th century. The inn was originally called The
Bakers Arms, a name it kept until 1898, when it became The Bullers Arms.
The name was taken from Redvers Buller, Commander-in-Chief in South
Africa, and known as 'The Man Of The Hour' following his success in the
relief of Ladysmith during the Boer War.

During the reign of Queen Victoria the inn was rebuilt following its
destruction by a fire which swept through Chagford. In 1950 the smaller

rooms which occupied what is now the public bar were made into one room. Hanging from the wooden beam which runs along the centre of the ceiling is an assortment of brass and copperware, including coal scuttles, water pitchers and a large stew pot. The walls are adorned with a collection of military plaques.

9: Burrator Inn

On the B3212 road 1.25 miles from Yelverton,
4.5 miles from Princetown. Tel: Yelverton (0822) 853121

The Burrator Inn comprises a spacious lounge/public bar, restaurant and dining room and is sited on the edge of the moor, a mile from the Burrator Reservoir from which it now takes its name.

Since it was first built in 1880, the inn, formerly the Manor Hotel, has seen many changes, both to the building itself and the surrounding area. The original building was not quite as large as it is today, the interior was made up of small rooms leading off a passageway that ran along where the bar is situated. At one end was the Spanish Bar (now the dining room) and at the other end, and just around the corner, was the village Post Office. The Post Office closed down in 1959 and this is now the games area for pool and darts.

The extension now housing the restaurant was added in 1910, this was at first used as the public bar before being converted into its present use in 1984. It was in 1960 that the name of the inn was changed from the Manor Hotel.

Photograph copied with permission of Mrs Wallbank

The former Plymouth and Princetown Railway, which ceased running in 1957, used to pass by at the rear, stopping at the Dousland Halt station situated on the opposite side of the inn's car park.

It is rumoured that just after the turn of the century a young baby was murdered on the premises, and on various occasions residents sleeping in the rooms on the top floor have mentioned feeling an eerie presence. Forty years ago a young disabled boy who was confined to a wheelchair said that he had seen a lady dressed in black with an assortment of keys hanging from a belt around her waist.

10: Carpenters Arms

In the Village of Ilsington, 3 miles from Bovey Tracey
and 1 mile from Haytor Vale. Tel: Haytor (0364) 661215

It is thought that The Carpenters Arms dates back to the 17th century, originally starting as a farmhouse belonging to Court Barton Farm. The date when it first became an inn is uncertain, although there is a record which shows that there was an auction held at The Carpenters Arms on 15 July 1817.

Originally the inn had just the public bar with the entrance at the front. At the rear of the building and running parallel with the church path was a lean-to shed which in the early days was a blacksmith's shop, stables and outside toilet. The landlord in 1870 was George Tarr and he was also the local blacksmith. When the smithy and stables closed these outbuildings were fully incorporated into the main structure. A rear door gave access into a small passageway at the end of which was the 'bottle and jug' where customers were served through a hatchway. On the left of the passage was a door which opened into the landlord's sitting room and on the right a door which gave access to a small lounge bar.

In 1957 the main entrance door at the end of the building was fitted, and in 1979 the interior was completely refurbished when landlord Bill Williams removed part of the original wall of the building separating the public and lounge bars, as well as the walls forming the passageway, thus extending the lounge into what was formerly his sitting room. This also enabled the building of the interior toilets which eliminated the journey out through the front door and up the church path to the outdoor toilets. At some time in the past the original fireplace had been replaced with a Devon grate, this was removed and the beautiful large, open fireplace was restored to its former glory, complete with a cloam oven which had been filled in with bricks and rubble.

In the early 1920s a few of the local lads who regularly frequented the inn were out doing a spot of late-night rabbit shooting when they saw a large bird in the trees. Thinking that it was a pheasant, one of them, called 'Chappie' Yeo, took a shot at it and killed it. When they went to collect it, they found that it was not a pheasant after all but a peacock, and the only peacock they knew of in this area was the one belonging to the local vicar, Parson Patch. They decided amongst themselves that they had better keep quiet over the matter and Chappie Yeo took it home where his Mother buried it. Parson Patch posted a ten shilling reward for information concerning his lost peacock and one day when he appeared at the bottle and jug to buy some ale he was spotted by our group of lads who were sitting in the corner of the bar. One of them 'Lordy' Roberts shouted over, 'Parson it was Chappie Yeo who shot your peacock', to which the parson replied 'He would not do that', and promptly bought Chappie a pint (little did he know!).

11: The Castle Inn

In the Village of Lydford, 1 mile from the A386.
Tel: Lydford (082282) 242

The early 16th century Castle Inn was originally the home of the Keeper of the nearby castle, before becoming, for a short period of time, a farmhouse. Later on it served a dual purpose, being also an ale house. The farmer's wife would sell cider and beer while her husband tended to the farm. The farming side eventually disappeared leaving a 'local' public house in Lydford which was first known as the White Horse Inn. It kept this name until 1807 when it became the Castle Inn. Originally there was just the one bar, the Tinners' Bar, where you can now see a unique collection of antique posters of stallions.

In 1964 Rachael and Jim Beesley became the landlords and it was not long before they became curious as to why the walls of the building were about six feet thick. After a little exploratory digging at the plaster they discovered in the Tinners' Bar the large fireplace and oven which can be seen today. It is thought that just outside the door that leads from this bar to the gent's toilet there used to be a deep well that had been filled-in some time prior to Rachael and Jim taking over the inn.

The right-hand side of the building was taken up with a sitting room and tea room. These were converted in 1966 into the Foresters' Bar. There was also a large fireplace discovered here beneath the plaster. This beautiful granite fireplace is said to date back to the time of the Normans. As this inn was not built until the 16th century this fireplace must have been sited elsewhere before being moved to its present position. During the winter months, large logs can be seen ablaze in it while in the summer it is filled

Photograph - Chapman & Son - 1906

with a profusion of brightly-coloured flowers. Above it there are seven Lydford Pennies dating from the reign of Ethelred The Unready (circa AD 1000) when Lydford was an important borough of Devon with its own mint

Separating these rooms from the Tinners' Bar was a stone walled and floored passageway which ran from the front entrance of the building, straight through to the back door. This was known as the horse passage; customers arriving at the inn on horseback would dismount at the front door and then lead their horse along the passageway to the yard at the rear.

Until 1967 the landlords had an additional responsibility to being a publican. They were paid a small annual fee to look after the daily upkeep of the castle itself, making sure that the grass was cut and everything was kept shipshape. The Castle Inn would also hold an annual harvest festival, organised by the landlord, including a service conducted by the local preacher followed by an auction where the proceeds from gifts received would be handed over to a charity.

Many years ago a stranger riding a white horse stopped at the inn requesting shelter for the night from the storm that was raging. After stabling his horse he entered the inn and while he was warming himself near the open fire, a local asked him from which direction he had travelled. He replied that he had come from Brent Tor along the road to Lydford. 'That is impossible', the local replied, 'For the bridge over the gorge has been washed away.' To this news the stranger went ghostly white, when he remembered how, in the darkness, his horse had jumped without warning. Not knowing it at the time, the horse had saved his life.

LYDFORD CASCADE.

12: *The Church House Inn*

4.5 miles from Ashburton, 3.5 miles from Buckfastleigh
on the southeast edge of Dartmoor. Tel: Poundsgate 208

In the past there was nearly always a 'Church House' inn in each village or town. Sometimes they were run by people of the church, who would brew the ale for the village on the premises, the proceeds from its sale being used for the upkeep of the local church. Such inns were used as resting places for travelling monks or priests, and were nearly always close to the church.

The Church House Inn at Holne was built in 1329 and was at first a priest's house. It was a single storey building with thick granite walls and a thatched roof. At the right-hand side of the building was a stable, now part of the public bar. The date when it became a public house is uncertain but it has belonged to the church since 1742 and the rent goes to support of the church. When it first became a public house it was known as the Tavistock Inn.

During the 15th century the first floor was added along with the porchway, which at that time had a window of ecclesiastical design. The main room now called the Kingsley Room (named after the famous author, Charles Kingsley, who was born nearby at the vicarage and whose well-known books include *Westward Ho!* and *The Water Babies*), has a beautiful internal oak screen which was fitted around the year 1530, there is also a long, curved bench-seat made of elm, added in the 18th century. There is an open fireplace which gives the room a very cosy feeling.

Photo reproduced by permission of Mr. Bevan.

About 1800 the name of the inn was changed to Church House Inn. Just over a hundred years later, between 1908-1925 the roof of the building was raised and, in 1925, the woodwork on the porchway was added and the old window replaced. It is said that Oliver Cromwell stayed at the inn during the battle of Totnes in the Civil War, and more recently the former Archbishop of Canterbury, Dr Ramsey, enjoyed the hospitality of the inn.

13: The Cleave

In the Village of Lustleigh, 3 miles from Bovey Tracey.
Tel: Lustleigh (06477) 223

The beautiful thatched Cleave Inn dates from the 15th century. It was originally the main farm building of Lustleigh Farm and the cottages surrounding the picturesque village green also belonged to the farm.

It is thought that there was a consecrated chapel below the roof on the second floor, but there is no remaining evidence of this today. The monks attached to Buckfast Abbey used the upstairs room as a place of prayer on the occasions when they stayed at the inn, so there may well have been a chapel here many years ago.

It wasn't until the early 1920s that the farmhouse became a hotel and finally an inn. The landlady, Mrs Scott Painter, ran the hotel for just over forty years. During this time, today's front lounge was the residents' dining room and the restaurant was the owner's sitting room. The rear lounge was the public bar, mainly used by the local farm workers. This bar was also a waiting room for travellers using the nearby railway, the station only being 200 yards away. Unfortunately the railway was closed in 1961.

Reproduced with permission of Mrs. Perring,
showing inn behind left of engine.

The open fireplace in the front lounge bar was discovered in the 1950s, revealing an oak beam and bread oven.

14: Cornwood Inn

In the Village of Cornwood 5 miles from Ivybridge
and 3 miles from Lee Mill. Tel: Plymouth (0752) 837225

The date when the Cornwood Inn was built is unknown. The first real evidence of a public house here is on a tithe map dated 1841, which shows a Tavistock Inn on this site. There are records that show licensed victuallers in Cornwood as far back as 1761. It wasn't until 1873 that the inn changed its name to Cornwood Inn.

There have been many alterations to the building over the years. What undoubtedly was a small structure to start with, has been enlarged over the years. At the time when William Sandover was landlord, 1930-1939, Kelly's Directory of Devonshire lists The Cornwood Inn as having a tea garden and tennis courts, since replaced by a car park.

Thirty years ago the rear of the building was extended. This enlarged the lounge bar and allowed a restaurant to be added. Along what was the original wall of the lounge there is a large open fireplace and it is thought that there might possibly be a small baker's oven hidden behind the plaster further along this wall towards the front of the building. The smaller 'village' bar, where the pool table can be found, is also thought to have a fireplace hidden somewhere along the outer wall.

15: Dartmoor Inn (Lydford)

On the A386, midway between Okehampton and Tavistock at junction with the road to Lydford. Tel: Lydford (082282) 221

There has been an inn on this site for at least 700 years, serving the needs of packhorse drivers and mounted travellers passing between the north and south of Devon. The present inn dates from the 16th century, the beer-cellar

still having the original roughly hewn tree trunk beams. At one time there was just the front bar, which has been extended over the years. The landlord's sitting room was turned into the back bar in 1966. Further improvements have taken place since and recently the inn has been completely redecorated, keeping its original character: low ceilings, wood panelling covering most of the thick granite walls, and massive open fireplaces, in one of which is a village scene with the miniature dolls and animals made from raffia. The original open veranda has been enclosed and made into a delightful sun lounge.

In each of the side walls of the porchway there used to be a small opening (now closed up, but still evident). When a convict had escaped from the prison at nearby Princetown, a policeman could sit in the porch and keep watch for the escapee.

THE DARTMOOR INN, LYDFORD, DEVON.

Reproduced with permission of Mr. P. Hyde

Between 1963-1977, John Morgan, who was the landlord at the time, bought a further six premises and formed a group of inns all bearing the word Dartmoor in their name. These all used to show the same sign. In addition to the Dartmoor Inn Lydford, there was the Dartmoor Union Halberton, the Old Dartmor Inn Halwell, the Dartmoor Halfway Inn Bickington, the Dartmoor Maiden Maidencombe, and the Dartmoor Railway Inn at Crediton.

Along with his group of inns, Mr Morgan, who was well known as a jovial character, became famous for his speciality form of pub grub known as 'Grotty Nosh'. This unusual form of food, and its name, first came on the scene during the very bad winter of 1963, when a group of Royal Marines, who had been stranded on the moor in a snowstorm, made their way to the Dartmoor Inn. On their arrival they asked Mr Morgan if he could provide them with a hot meal. Being a little low on provisions he went into the kitchen and emptied the contents of an assortment of tins, and anything else he could lay his hands on, into a large pot. When he served up this 'stew' one of the marines looked up after tasting a mouthful and said 'what grotty nosh!'

It was at this inn that Salvation Yeo, bosun to Captain Amos Leigh, slew the King of the Gubbins. The Gubbins were a family of small, ginger-haired rogues who lived nearby in Lydford Gorge, about 300 years ago. This band of villains has been immortalised in Charles Kingsley's book *Westward Ho!*.

There is an unknown ghost who likes to pay a visit to each new landlord during the first two weeks of his tenancy. Just after Paul, the present landlord, took over the inn he turned on a tap and found that his water supply had stopped. He tried to sort out the problem with no success, so he enlisted the help of Chris Paget, the previous landlord who lived next door. Together they checked out the water pipes, tracing them back up into the loft, where they found the header tank bone dry. While Paul searched around in the loft he overheard Chris, who was sitting on the edge of the tank say 'Please leave him alone, he's a decent sort of chap, give him a break'. Within seconds the water started to flow again.

Could this be a coincidence or had the ghost had enough fun?

16: Dartmoor Inn (Merrivale)

Beside the B3357 at Merrivale, 2 miles from Princetown.

Tel: Princetown 340

The Dartmoor Inn is made up of four or five cottages dating from the 17th Century. When it first became an inn it was just the main cottage (tallest building in the old photo). The inn was most probably a coaching stop as the small building on the left is thought to have been the stables. This was raised in height and incorporated into the inn around the year 1920, with the cottages on the right being enlarged and added before the start of the Second World War. The dividing walls were removed in the 1970s to make the long through-bar with its wooden beamed ceiling seen today. The large inglenook fireplace was a domestic fireplace before being enlarged with granite from the nearby Merrivale quarry in the 1950s.

The inn receives its water supply from the Sortridge and Grimstone leat. It is stored in seven large tanks in the loft, before being filtered and treated with ultra-violet light.

The earliest record of there being an inn here is on a census form dated 30 March 1841, which lists the occupants of the cottages and their occupations. It shows John Harding as stonemason and innkeeper.

Photo: Valentine

At the turn of the century the population of the neighbourhood was far greater than today and, as a result, the inn was a very important and busy place, with local trade coming from the nearby quarrymen's cottages and farms. After a night of merriment they would make their way home by lamplight, on foot or horseback, in different directions across the moor, singing and calling to each other as they went.

During the 1950s the front outer walls of the inn were covered with slate shingles (see photo). Thankfully they were removed after a short space of time. It was around this time that the inn doubled as a petrol station, this side of the business ceasing in the early 1960s. The inn has been immortalized in Eden Philpott's book *Mother* in which it is called 'The Huntsman'. Many locations in the area can be recognised under different names in the book.

The Gilders and Colts Association from Tavistock, annually hold an event known as the 'opening up' of the moor. This takes place on the 1 March, when they walk up from their home town to this inn (replenishing their strength with pasties and ale), before continuing on to Peter Tavy. Their proclamation reads:

> *Whereas, on the first Sunday of March in the year of our Lord 1950, there was assembled at this their birthplace, that most excellent and worshipful company of Gilders of the township of Tavistock.*
>
> *And whereas on that day and to mark the occasion of their twenty sixth episcopal tour, my Lord Bishop of the said company of Gilders, with keen eye, noble purpose and raised axe, did smite all that piece of wall which heretofore did stand, and so make a way where there was none before.*
>
> *It is hereby proclaimed that this shall henceforth be known as 'Bishops Way' and here for all time, free men shall pass upon their lawful occassions to the further upholding of the democratic way of life, to the pride and satisfaction of the people of Devon and glory of the British flag.*
>
> *God Save The Queen!*

This proclamation can be seen on the wall at the beginning of the passageway (Bishops Way)) which leads to the small bar and toilets.

Reproduced with permission of Mr D. Green

A few years ago the inn was taken over by the BBC along with many well known personalities, including Lady Sayer, Ian Mercer and Michael Burke, their interest being ghosts and the supernatural on Dartmoor. There have been a few unaccountable events here. Once, when Gerald, a fine old gentleman who has been a local here for many years, went to the back of the building, he felt an icy presence, but no one was to be seen. This caused the hairs on the back of his neck to stand on end, and to this day he will not go back there. This unseen ghost has for some reason been given the name of 'Mary'. There has also been the sighting of another ghost by guests staying at the inn. This is said to be the spirit of a young girl who had died at the turn of the century. She walks the length of the upstairs corridor, not bothering to open the doors, just walking through them.

17: Devil's Elbow

In the centre of Princetown on the B3212 Two Bridges Yelverton Road.
Tel: Princetown (082289)

The Devil's Elbow is situated beside the main Two Bridges to Plymouth Road at Princetown. It was built in 1827 and was originally called The Railway Inn, as this is where the horse-drawn Plymouth and Dartmoor Railway had its terminus. The horses were stabled in what is now the 'stable bar'. The inn was also used as a store for the railway company.

One of the first landlords was Mr J. Rowe, who as well as being the landlord, doubled as the village dentist, which certainly had its benefits; you could either get drunk (local anaesthetic) and have a tooth pulled or have a tooth pulled and then get drunk to dull the pain, or both!

The name of the inn was changed to its present name around 1957, most probably taken from the tricky S-bend on the approach road to Princetown from Plymouth near Devil's Bridge.

18: Devon Tors

Beside the Green, Yelverton 9 miles from Plymouth.
Tel: Yelverton (0822) 853604

The Devon Tors is not how you might imagine a Dartmoor inn to appear. In fact it is more in keeping with places like Blackpool. It was originally three houses that were part of a terrace built in 1891 and known as Beech Villas, joined along the front by a conservatory. In 1910 they were bought by Charles Wilson, a gentleman who was a strict churchman, and he converted it into a temperance hotel. Yelverton at that time was very popular as a place for convalescence as the air was thought to be very pure.

The hotel was a popular place to stay and with Mr Wilson's religious beliefs, and the Yelverton Church nearby, it came as no surprise when some of the hotel's guests donated a brass crucifix to the church. In 1962 the hotel was granted a full licence and seven years later, in 1969, a buttery was opened. The hotel finally closed in 1982 with the main section of the building being converted into flats. The bar of the premises, which occupied the ground floor, remained as the Devon Tors Inn and was extended in 1984 with the acquisition of the buttery which had just closed.

The grass verge surrounding the inn's car park is part of the embankment on which a section of the horse-drawn Plymouth and Dartmoor Railway ran. A spur line ran from in front of the Methodist church to the North Devon Wharf (canal terms were still in use for some railway buildings, stations, etc.), where the Yelverton Garage is now situated.

19: Drewe Arms

In the Village Square of Drewsteignton,
1 mile from the A30 at Crockernwell. Tel: Drewsteignton (0647) 21224

When you enter this beautiful 16th century, thatch roofed inn, you take a step back in time. This is how many of the inns on the moor first started for, apart from the changing of its name, things here have not changed over the passing of the years.

The inn occupies the section of the building to the left of the entrance door, there is no large conventional lounge/public bar, pool tables or one-armed bandits here. What we have is a tap room at the rear, and in the front a small room which serves as a bar. Here the stone floor where the dart players stand has, over the years, developed quite a groove. The inn was originally called the New Inn, then in 1873 it became the Druids Arms and then just before the First World War it became The Drewe Arms, following the arrival of the Drewe family to the area. This necessitated the making of a new sign showing the coat of arms of the Drewe Family. A young lad from the village was dispatched by pony and trap to Yeoford Station to collect it, but instead of the normal sign made of wood he found a very heavy sign made of cast iron with a wrought iron frame. Mr J. C. Drewe, head of a wealthy merchant family, had Castle Drogo built at Drewsteignton in 1911, as the family home. It was the last 'castle' to be built in England.

The main section of the Drewe Arms is the home of the landlady, Mabel Mudge, she is a wonderful woman in her nineties who is affectionately known as 'Auntie' to everyone. Because of her age she cannot get around very much now and it is her 'helpers', as they are known, that look after the customers. The Mudge family has looked after the inn for nearly 100 years.

Mabel's brother-in-law Alfred Mudge was the first when he became the landlord in 1906. 'Auntie' came to the Inn in 1919 with her husband Ernest Mudge after they had been licensees at the Judge Jeffreys Inn at Crockernwell. Ernest Mudge died in 1971 and since then Mabel has run it herself!

20: East Dart Hotel

Postbridge on the B3212
Tel: (0822) 88213

The East Dart Hotel was built in the early 19th century, originally as an inn, though shortly after, in the mid 1800s it became a temperance hotel selling nothing stronger than lemonade. This followed a strange occurrence when

Lizzie (a devoted churchgoer) wife of landlord John Webb had just returned from church where she had heard a sermon by the local preacher emphasizing the evils of strong drink. She relentlessly badgered her husband into getting rid of all of his ale and spirits, this he did by rolling the beer barrels down to the East Dart river late one evening and emptying them. While this was happening, a little further downstream, a black dog, which had strayed over from Moretonhampstead, was taking a drink from the river. Shortly after satisfying his thirst the dog began to howl at the moon, (maybe by now he was seeing double). The ghost of this dog has been seen from time to time making the journey from Moretonhampstead to Postbridge, still trying to satisfy his thirst.

When a temperance hotel

The hotel remained temperance for 75 years before changing its name to The East Dart Hotel in the late 1920s, it was at this time that alcohol was once again sold on the premises.

The inn is a renowned meeting place for huntsmen, being ideally situated in the centre of four hunting areas. Each year up to fifteen hunts start from the inn's car park. The large 'Huntsman's Bar', with its wooden beamed ceiling has a mural spanning two walls depicting the events of a hunt from beginning to end.

21: Elephant's Nest

In the Hamlet of Horndon, 1 mile from Mary Tavy.
Tel: Mary Tavy (0822) 810273

One thing that you would not expect to see on Dartmoor, or anywhere else for that matter, is an elephant's nest! Well, there is one. It is a 16th century inn situated in the Hamlet of Horndon, not far from the beautiful Tavy Cleave.

The building was originally three miners' cottages, later joined together to make a farmhouse. When this became an inn, just after the turn of this century, it was called the New Inn, since the village already had an inn (The Black Lion).

In 1952 the name was changed to The Elephant's Nest, a name arrived at when customers used to taunt the somewhat overweight landlord, saying that he looked 'an elephant on his nest'.

The first thing that you will notice as you enter the inn is the very low entrance door (the miners must have been small people). The public bar has a low beamed ceiling on which is displayed a large collection of bank notes from around the world. On the exposed stone wall at the far end there is an assortment of brass plates, including two that resemble beautifully decorated shields. They are in fact trays that used to carry bread and cakes. Along another wall there is a mural showing a jungle scene with five elephants.

There are two family rooms, one slightly larger than the other, both have low, beamed ceilings and large open fireplaces. When fires are lit during the cold winter months, they give out a great deal of heat, enhancing the already cosy atmosphere of the inn. Set into one wall in each of these rooms is a cupboard containing a large collection of china elephants. In 1930 an extension was added to the building, now housing a kitchen and extra bedroom.

22: Exeter Inn

In West Street, Ashburton.
Tel: Ashburton (0364) 52013

The Exeter Inn is the oldest public house in Ashburton, having been built in 1131 to house the men building the original church in Ashburton. It then became a 'church house' before finally becoming an inn. The building was partially rebuilt in 1585. The inn was frequently used by Sir Francis Drake on his many journeys from Plymouth to Queen Elizabeth's court in London.

Until 1965 the Inn consisted of four separate smaller bar rooms, two on either side of a passage leading from the main entrance at the front to the back door and secluded beer garden at the rear. There used to be stables situated at the rear and customers visiting the inn would lead their horses along the passage through the building to reach them. The walls forming the sides of the passage were removed in 1965, thus forming the larger public and lounge bars, both having wood-burning fires. The drinks dispensing area of the bar is incorporated into the now disused former fireplace, the sides of which are made from two old mill stones.

In June 1991 the interior was completely refurbished, and with its low ceilings, open log fires and atmospheric lighting, it still retains its original character. A new roof was fitted at this time, and in the loft space was found a number of interesting items including a button from a Napoleonic uniform, part of a clay pot with the date 1799 on it, and several clay pipes with different designs on the bowls. There were also two pairs of shoes thought to be between 200-300 years old; one pair being for a very small child and the other slightly larger.

During the month of July, an ancient traditional ceremony takes place in the Chapel of St Lawrence. This is the election of the new Portreeve (Bailiff). This event dates back to Saxon times and used to be held in the Exeter Inn. It is at this time that the Bread Weighers and Ale Tasters are appointed; the Ale Tasters then do a round of the inns. Many years ago (when the Ale Tasters wore leather breeches), they would pour a little ale on to a seat, then sit on it. If their breeches stuck to the seat, the ale failed to pass the test. Punishment for the landlord was a fine, or he could find himself having the ale poured over him.

1991 Ale Tasting ceremony - Landlord Jim McNichol, Ale Tasters, Fred Miners and Philip Pool

23: Fleece and Firkin

St Lawrence Street, Ashburton.
Tel: Ashburton (0364) 52382

When the inn first opened in 1825 it was known as the Old Bottle Inn. It was smaller than it is now, being only the straight section of the building before it curves around the corner. The inn was expanded in 1868 when a deal was agreed to exchange pieces of land between the landlord and the South Devon Railway, who planned to open a branch line between Totnes and Ashburton. The railway owned the piece of land the landlord needed to expand the inn, while the landlord owned the land required by the railway to build their station.

The name of the inn was changed to the Railway Inn when the line reached Ashburton on 1 May 1872. The South Devon Railway continued to serve Ashburton until 1967 when it was closed following the construction of the A30 dual carriageway which effectively cut the line in two. On the 15 October 1927 the inn was bought by the Courage Brewery for £1550.

In 1973 when Jack Billings was the landlord, the name of the inn was changed once more to the Silent Whistle, an apt name following the demise of the railway. During the fifteen years that Jack was the landlord a challenge was set to anyone who could climb one of the two seventeen feet high poles in the public bar that reached from floor to ceiling. The climb had to be achieved one-handed with a half pint of beer in the other. On reaching the top and having touched the ceiling with their head, the climber would drink the half pint of beer before descending to the floor where he would win £1 for his efforts. Only five people managed this, one of them being Reg (Pop) Distin and he was 70 years old when he did it!

The inn was closed down in 1985 for two years and it was during this time that it was completely refurbished, before opening in 1987 as the Fleece and Firkin. The interior walls are partially covered in wood panels that were once fitted in a church, as was the beautifully carved screen behind and above the bar.

24: Forest Inn

Situated: 1 mile from the Ashburton-Two Bridges Road at Hexworthy.

Tel: Poundsgate (03643) 208

The Forest Inn, which was built in the mid 19th century, overlooks beautiful views of some of Dartmoor's finest scenery, with Yar Tor and Corndon Tor on the distant horizon, and the West Dart river in the valley below.

The inn is owned by the Royal Duchy of Cornwall, Dartmoor's largest landlord (the Prince of Wales' feathers can been seen on the outside wall).

Originally the inn was thatched (see photo) but unfortunately it was almost completely destroyed by fire in 1913. A small section of the building survived and this can be seen on the right of the new structure (see photo) which was completed in 1916. More recently the remainder of the original building was removed and the premises extended to today's size.

Before 1913

Rebuilt 1916

The Forest Inn was favourite haunt of William Crossing the famous Dartmoor guide and author. Many a night he spent here, after his journeys out on to the Moor, sometimes returning to the inn very late at night after everyone else had gone to bed and then asking the landlord for a hot meal.

There are several interesting items of ironwork to be seen outside the inn, including a man-trap, which many years ago is said to have been placed outside the prison at Princetown.

25: Fox and Hounds Hotel

On the A386 Okehampton-Tavistock Road below the village of Sourton.
Tel: Lydford (082 282) 206

The Fox and Hounds Hotel has been included in this book, because it started out as an inn. The original Fox and Hounds Inn was built in the 18th century and is the small white building situated on the left of the main part of today's hotel. This has now become the private accommodation of the proprietors, with the exception of one room, which has been made into the pool room. The old low-beamed ceiling and thick granite walls have been retained, as well as the large open fireplace, retaining much of its original character. The old barn has since been converted into a skittle alley. Like the Bearslake Inn a little way up the road towards Okehampton, it was part of the Leawood Estate, owned by Lt-Colonel Calmady Hamlyn.

Photo by Tom Quick Reproduced with permission of Mr Ward

The main part of today's hotel was built around the turn of the century. On the side of the bar there is a large mural depicting a fox hunt in full chase, painted by Willie Brandt who was a German prisoner of war, held at the nearby prison camp towards the end of the Second World War.

In the lounge bar there are two tables, made from the bases of antique sewing machines. Behind the bar, in the centre of the shelf, there is a fine model of the hotel made from matchsticks, this was made by Charlie Butterworth in 1986.

The bridlepath which runs close to the hotel gives access to one of the most beautiful parts of the moor, with Arms Tor, Brat Tor and Great Nodden being within easy reach.

26: George Inn

On the outskirts of Buckfastleigh, close to Lower Dean and the A38 dual carriageway. Tel: Buckfastleigh (0364) 42708

The George Inn is an amalgamation of a series of cottages dating from the 18th century, although it was not until the 19th century that it first became an inn. Originally known as the Half Moon, it was a bustling coaching inn, being ideally situated beside the main Plymouth to Exeter road. The name of the inn was changed to the George Inn before becoming the Stable Door Inn in the early 1970s. The landlord at that time, Mr Kelly, owned some racehorses, one of which won the Irish Grand National. It was at this time that the inn was enlarged with the addition of the section now housing the Ship Room. In this room there is a large encased model of H.M.S. 'The

George' a replica of the original 'Royal George', a man o' war with 100 guns. She was the sister ship of Admiral Nelson's flagship 'Victory' and was built in 1746 at Woolwich. She took ten years to build and was constructed from approximately 2500 oak trees, each being about 100 years old. After 26 years' service she was caught in a sudden storm off Portsmouth in August 1782 and sank.

In October 1984 the inn closed its doors to business for 18 months before re-opening and reverting back to one of its former names The George Inn. Along with the Ship Room the inn contains the main bar, Queen's lounge and games room. Separating the main bar from the Queen's lounge is a partition wall incorporating a fireplace built into a beautiful tunnel.

27: Globe Inn

In the centre of Buckfastleigh.
Tel: Buckfastleigh (0364) 42223

The Globe Inn is a former coaching inn dating from the early 17th century. The large double doors along the side of the building used to give access to the stables situated at the rear. In 1966 plans were suggested for the removal of Weech Corner on which the inn stands. The Globe was to close and have its business transferred to the Valiant Soldier. These proposals for road alterations never materialised and ironically it was the Valiant Soldier that went out of business. For many years, during the evenings, the local policeman would stand on Weech Corner, being more or less in the centre of the town, and from here he could survey the immediate area as the public houses closed. It was said that in the 1950s, he would always know when it was closing time as he would be able to hear Freddie Hawkins, the barman of the King's Arms, call time.

28: Globe Inn

In the centre of Chagford, opposite the Church.
Tel: Chagford (0647) 433485

The Globe Inn is a 16th century coaching inn, originally named The Gregory's Arms, and as far as is known it has always been an inn. There is a lounge bar, public bar (both complete with large fireplaces), restaurant and residents' lounge. The fireplace in the lounge was discovered in 1981 when others were being removed.

It was proposed in the last century that a direct railway link be made to Chagford. This however never came to be and all connections to Exeter and Moretonhampstead were made, at first by horse-drawn coaches and then, on the 1 June 1904, with motor coaches. These left from directly in front of the Globe Inn.

The bungalow at the rear of the inn was formerly the stables for the spare horses required by the coaches. Also at the rear was a large coopering works and hogsheads for cider and beer were made here. There was also an industry in quart firkins for farm labourers to carry their cider in.

The inn is thought to be haunted by the ghost of a chambermaid who was accused of witchcraft. She was tried by being strapped in a chair and lowered into the river. The fact that she drowned proved that she was innocent according to the law of those times! Various guests staying in the Azalea Room on the first floor (all the rooms are named after flowers) have said that they have felt a strange eerie presence.

29: Golden Lion

East Street, Ashburton.
Tel: Ashburton (0364) 52205

The Golden Lion is a large brick built building dating from 1768. It was originally a mansion house built for Nicholas Tripe, a surgeon in Ashburton. It first became an inn in 1795 and was at that time one of two Golden Lions in East Street. The older, original, Golden Lion Inn, which was also owned by Mr Tripe, was built in the 1600s and closed in 1797. It is now the National Westminster Bank. During the 1800s, the Golden Lion became a busy coaching inn and the coaches that ran twice daily between Exeter and Plymouth Docks would stop here en route.

The Golden Lion has been strongly linked over the years with various political parties. In 1825 William Barons became the landlord, he supported the Tory Party and had strong political views backed up by a private army of 'heavies'. By fair means or foul he tried to ensure victory for his party.

On 23 July 1837 he became directly involved with a riot that took place outside the inn which at that time was being used as the headquarters for the local Tory candidate. George Knowling, a Liberal supporter, had been abducted by the 'heavies' and driven twenty miles away across Dartmoor and abandoned. Fortunately some of Mr Knowling's friends had followed him and brought him back to Ashburton where they triumphantly paraded him in front of the Golden Lion. This then erupted into a full scale riot between supporters from both parties. In 1856 the name of the inn was changed slightly when it became the Golden Lion Hotel, and in 1940 it was rented out for a short time as a school.

In 1990 it became the headquarters of the Monster Raving Looney Party and they now hold their annual conference there. Today's landlord, Alan Hope, who took over the hotel in 1978 is a staunch supporter of the party and in 1987 became the first member ever to be elected as a Town Councillor.

It is reputed that in 1901 Sir Arthur Conan-Doyle stayed at the hotel for a few days whilst he was touring Dartmoor on holiday. During his stay, he visited Foxtor Mire which he later renamed Grimpen Mire and incorporated it into his famous novel *The Hound of the Baskervilles.*

30: Highwaymans Inn

Beside the A386, at Sourton, 5.5 miles from Okehampton.
Tel: Okehampton (0837) 86243

The Highwaymans Inn dates back to the 12th century, although when it first became an inn is uncertain. It is thought to be have been an alehouse in 1280. Many years later it became a coaching inn, being ideally situated beside the old turnpike road between Okehampton and Tavistock. In 1620 it was known as The Golden Fleece. It then changed to the Highwaymans Inn in November 1961.

The Inn has been imaginatively transformed from stables, barn, kitchen and pump house, after a lot of hard work by Buster and Rita Jones. The interior has undergone a complete transformation, and is now an Aladdin's Cave of dimly lit rooms and passageways.

To enter the inn you have to step inside a coach forming the doorway, parts of which came from one of the original coaches used on the Okehampton to Launceston Road. Incorporated into the ceiling is a wheel from an old coach. The door on the left leads into the Coach Cabin Lounge which has stone walls and floor and a large oak beam supporting a wooden ox plough. Adorning the walls are many items of horse livery as well as a large Scottish ceremonial brass shield. Placed near the fireplace is an antique metal cheese press. The passage in the corner of this room, towards the front of the building, leads into the Rita Jones Locker Bar which was formerly the stables and barn. This now resembles a cabin aboard an old sailing galleon, with its wooden floor and ceiling. The oak beamed ceiling is supported in the centre by a wooden post with a large wheel at the top (obtained from an old round house). Placed around the walls are booths separated by low wooden bannisters which, accompanied by the subdued lights, give a touch of cosiness. In front of the booths are old capstans which have been converted into glass topped tables filled with treasure. The wood for the ceiling, floor and bannisters was obtained from a chapel in Okehampton which had been demolished.

Photo 1963 Reproduced With Permission of Landlady.

Going back to the passage just inside the entrance door, the door on the right leads into the stone walled and floored Hideaway Bar. This was the main part of the original inn. The large root of an old oak tree has been incorporated into the wall and this supports the dart board. In the front window bay, the table is made from bellows obtained from a blacksmith's shop. Other antiques include a wooden cheese press and wool winder.

Above the entrance to the low tunnel, which used to be the pump house, is the head of the last working ox in the area, one of a pair of oxen which had won first prize on the Bridestowe Estate. The head was presented to Buster Jones by Reg Ellis whose father had passed it on to him. The tunnel has sometimes been referred to as the Tunnel of Love. To the left and down the steps is a glass-floored grotto housing a collection of stuffed wildlife.

The wood used to make the bar tops in each of the bars is from oak trees that had been dragged from bogs on the Moor. Built on to the outside of the Rita Jones Locker Bar is a children's room designed to look like an old woman's boot.

31: Kestor Inn

In the village of Manaton, 4.5 miles from Bovey Tracey.
Tel: Manaton (057285) 204

The Kestor Inn was built in the early years of the century by Jim Hardy, a stonemason from Chagford, on behalf of the landlord of The Half Moon Inn on Manaton's picturesque village green. It was originally intended to be a boarding house for farm labourers and other workers in the area, but the landlord decided that Manaton did not really warrant two inns and closed down the Half Moon, favouring the size and position of the Kestor. It is thought that the inn arrived at its name because some of the granite used in its construction was brought over by the builder from the area of Kestor Rocks near Chagford.

The building was extended around 1980 with the addition of the family room, restaurant and games room. The walls surrounding the bar room are the original exterior walls of the building. The public bar with its oak-beamed ceiling has an unusual item situated in the corner nearest to the bar - an ornate fish pond, complete with small waterfall. The partitions between the backs of the seats along the wall nearest to the restaurant are made from old advertising boards which add a touch of nostalgia to the room.

The Kestor Inn sign proclaims it as being the Headquarters of the MCC, in this case Manaton Cricket Club!

32: Kings Arms

Fore Street, Buckfastleigh.
Tel: Buckfastleigh (0364) 42341

The 17th century Kings Arms is a former coaching inn situated beside the original Plymouth to Exeter Road. The stables, which housed the spare

horses required during the days of coach travel, were also used more recently when the Buckfastleigh Racecourse was in operation and some owners and trainers of racehorses would stay at the hotel.

One of the original upstairs rooms of the Kings Arms (now part of the National Westminster Bank) is where the first cinema pictures to be seen in Buckfastleigh were shown during 1919/20; customers paying one penny for the privilege. The local rugby team also used this room to hold their annual 'boiled pig's head' supper.

The Kings Arms is haunted by the ghost of a young girl who died tragically when she fell into the well situated in what is now the hallway leading from the main entrance. This was part of the courtyard when the Kings Arms was much smaller than today. She has been seen on various occasions, once by a gentleman just leaving the toilets! He saw her disappear through a wall.

33: Kings Arms

5 miles from Okehampton, at South Zeal
Tel: Okehampton (0837) 840300

The Kings Arms is thought to be approximately four hundred years old and stands beside the old Okehampton-Exeter trunk road in the village of South Zeal.

In the past the upper level of the inn was used as a hayloft and store for grain and corn. A reminder of this came twenty or so years ago when redecorating the bar. In removing the rough planking attached to the wooden beams in the ceiling, many wheelbarrow loads of grain had to be taken away. It was also at this time that a small open fireplace was enlarged, and the area of the bar which houses the dart board, formerly a cellar, was also redecorated to match the old world charm of the rest of the bar.

Up to forty years ago the inn was a cider house, selling its rough form of refreshment to the miners from the nearby Ramsey Copper Mine, and various tradesmen calling at the inn.

There are no stories of ghosts attached to this inn, in fact the landlady's mother, who was a well known psychic once said 'the inn has too much of a happy atmosphere to be the home of a ghost'.

34: Lantern Inn

Just off the Ashburton-Princetown Road, 1 mile from Ashburton.
Tel: Ashburton (0364) 52697

Since it was first built in 1913, originally as a gentleman's residence, the Lantern Inn has had a chequered history. It has been variously the Betweenways Hotel, the Grasshopper Night Club, the Lantern Hotel, and finally since 1990, the Lantern Inn.

The Lamplighters Bar is cosily lit with wall lamps and has a beamed ceiling which extends through into the Restaurant, added to the Inn in 1984. The large exposed stone fireplace was constructed in 1988 and this helps to give the room an 'olde worlde' atmosphere.

35: Leaping Salmon

In Horrabridge beside the River and near the Bridge,
3 miles from Tavistock. Tel: Yelverton (0822) 852939

The Leaping Salmon is made up from two cottages dating from 1746 and was originally known as The New Inn, a name it kept until 1951 when it changed to its present name. During 1945-46 it was known locally as 'The Starving Pig', a reference to the then landlord's pigs.

The inn consists of a split level open lounge and public bars complete with oak-beamed ceilings. In the public bar there is a large stone fireplace containing a wood-burning stove. The lounge has a small open stone fireplace and wood store set into the opposite wall. Until 1963 these rooms were separated by the wall dividing one of the original cottages from the other.

36: Leg o' Mutton

At Leg o' Mutton Corner, Yelverton, 9 miles from Plymouth.
Tel: Yelverton (0822) 854195

The exact date when the Leg o' Mutton was built is uncertain, records show that in 1846 it was a large house belonging to a Mr J. Williams. Mail was collected from here at 5.00am most mornings and taken by coach to Horrabridge. In 1882 it was sold to Julian Bayley who ran it as a temperance hotel until 1895. The hotel most probably replaced the Bullers

Arms that stood on the opposite side of the road and had been destroyed by fire in 1870.

In 1902 it was bought by Mr B. Meldrum who converted it back to a private dwelling before applying for and receiving permission to open it as a public house. It was known as the Yelverton Hotel. In the 1930s the building was acquired by Plymouth Breweries who continued to run it as the Yelverton Hotel until 1971 when it became The Foxhunter, the name being dedicated to the famous showjumper 'Foxhunter', owned by Colonel Harry Llewellyn, winner of a gold medal at the 1954 Helsinki Olympic Games. On 12 March 1979 Ken and Pat Middleton took over the inn and they changed the name once more on 1 April 1984 to its present name of Leg o' Mutton. The name is taken from an area of Yelverton in which the land is shaped like a leg of mutton.

37: London Inn

In West Street, Ashburton.
Tel: Ashburton (0364) 52478

The London Inn is a former coaching inn dating from the 15th century. In the days of travel by horse-drawn carriages this was a bustling place, being ideally sited beside the Plymouth to London turnpike road. Passengers would board and alight here whilst the horses were changed from the stables at the rear of the building.

The inn consists of two spacious bar areas separated by a thick exposed stone wall punctuated by two large openings. Up to 1980, when the inn was refurbished, these were doorways giving access to the then, separate bars. The two impressive stone fireplaces were restored to their original glory after having been covered-up and substituted by electric fires for many years. Placed around the walls and above the bar is an interesting collection of old rifles and pistols, while the oak-beamed ceiling is adorned with horse brasses. Joining on to the lower end of the bar and separated from it by a beautiful wrought iron screen, is the restaurant. Supporting the oak beams on the ceiling are two wooden pillars. The one in the centre of the room is placed upon an old mill stone, taken from the nearby Town Mill when it closed-down.

There are not many inns that have their own brewery on site. Thompson's ales was initiated by landlord Dan Thompson and his two sons Melvin and Rick in 1981. They used the room beside the ballroom on the first floor for the Brewery. Output at first was 200 gallons a week and 'Thompsons Bitter' was sold at 52p a pint, or you could get a discount if you bought it by the quart as the regulars would. Demand has increased and the brewery has now expanded and taken over the recently converted stables.

At the beginning of the 19th century, the surveyor with responsibility for maintaining the roads on Dartmoor was appointed at a ceremony held at the London Inn. Unfortunately, a horse was not provided, so to carry out his duties, he would have had to supply his own!

38: London Inn

In Horrabridge, 3 miles from Tavistock.
Tel: Yelverton (0822) 853567

The London Inn was created by amalgamating five cottages dating from the early 16th century and is a former coaching inn. The front section of the public bar was added in the early 1900s where there had originally been a courtyard. The stables situated at the rear of the building have since been converted into garages adjoining the inn's car park. The large fireplace, complete with cloam oven in the lounge bar is thought to be an original, having been built at the same time as the cottages.

39: London Inn

Beside the old A38 at South Brent.
Tel: South Brent (0364) 73223

The London Inn was built in the 19th century following the closure of the Clarence Inn sited on the opposite side of the road. In the early 1920s there used to be a cobbler's shop placed in the corner of the small public bar and many a 'local' who visited the inn would have his boots repaired at the same time. The inn also contained a small snug bar before it was enlarged in 1936 to almost double its original size with the addition of the spacious lounge bar seen today. Over the years the London Inn has been a popular stopping-off point for coach parties on their way to and from various occasions, since it is ideally sited beside the A38 Plymouth to Exeter Road.

40: Mary Tavy Inn

On the A386 Okehampton-Tavistock Road at Mary Tavy.
Tel: Mary Tavy (082281) 326

The 16th century Mary Tavy Inn has evolved from three cottages and used to be a stopping-off place for travellers making their way on the packhorse route between Okehampton and Tavistock. Over the years it has changed its name from the Elliott Hotel to the Bullers Arms and finally to its present name, around the turn of the century.

There used to be some more cottages in a row adjoining the inn, these have since been demolished. The occupant of one of these was the local blacksmith. This character met his untimely end at the gallows at nearby Gibbet Hill, his crime was that he was caught stealing sheep on the moor.

After his hanging he was buried in Mary Tavy churchyard.

The Coachman's Bar with its wooden beamed ceiling has a thatched canopy over the bar. The wall surrounding the open fire has many interesting items of brasswork, these include mouth bits from horse harnesses and many large keys.

If you sit in this bar and you happen to look up at the clock on the main ceiling beam, don't think that you have had too much to drink, and that the clock appears to be going the opposite way around. It is, it's an 'Irish' clock, made by Bernard Clark from Plymouth and was bought by the landlord in 1986.

The original open veranda has since been enclosed and is now the family room.

41: Northmore Arms

In the Hamlet of Wonson, 2.5 miles from Whiddon Down and .75 mile from Throwleigh. Tel: Okehampton (064723) 428

It it thought that the Northmore Arms was originally a labourer's cottage that also served as a cider house, before becoming an inn. At this time there were two separate rooms in the front of the inn. One of them being the bar room which was separated from the bar by a glazed partition, the cider and ale being served from a small hatchway on the right. The second room housed a piano and many a sing song was held here. Approximately twenty-five years ago the dividing wall was removed and the new bar was fitted.

Until the early 1970s the inn was known as The New Inn, when it changed its name to the Northmore Arms. The name being taken from the name of Mr Northmore who lived in the Manor House at the nearby Wonson Estate. He will go down in history as the gentleman who lost his estate at the turn of a card. It was during a game of cards that he gambled his estate and lost, beaten by the ace of diamonds. There is an engraving of this card on the wall of Wonson Manor for all to see today.

Over the years the inn has been locally known as 'The Wonson'. In fact there are still some people today who refer to it by this name.

42: The Old Inn

Just off the Village Green in the centre of Widecombe-in-the-Moor.
   Tel: Widecombe (03642) 207

The Old Inn, which was built in the 14th century, has been altered many times over the years. In 1977 the building was extensively damaged by fire. Most of the roof, first floor and part of the ground floor was destroyed. Thankfully the building has been restored to its former charm.

   The inn now consists of two lounges, a bar and restaurant, all aptly named after Widecombe Fair Folklore. There is the Widecombe Bar, Cobley Lounge and recently the former stables have been converted into The Old

Gray Mare Lounge. Each room has a large open fireplace and exposed granite walls.

The inn is said to have been haunted by two ghosts, one a man called Harry who was a local, and had been murdered on the premises. He had been sighted in the kitchen on various occasions until the fire in 1977, since then he has not been seen. The other, a young girl, has been heard crying in an upstairs bedroom. No one knows who this girl may be, it has been suggested that it could be the much heard of Kitty Jay, an 18th century orphan who hanged herself when she became pregnant by a landowner's son.

43: Oxenham Arms

In the Village of South Zeal, 5 miles from Okehampton.
Tel: Okehampton (0837) 840244

The Oxenham Arms was built in the 12th century by lay monks, although it was not until 1477 that it was first licensed. Not long after this it was almost completely rebuilt and became the dower house of The Burgoynes and then The Oxenham Family. The beautiful granite-walled inn has been constructed around a large granite menhir which is set into the wall of the snug bar and is said to be over 5000 years old. The bottom of this menhir has never been found, even though various people have dug down trying to find it, the last time being fifteen years ago when a depth of twenty-six feet was reached.

To enter the inn you pass through a beautiful porchway and thick oak door which leads into a flagstoned corridor that is part of the original building. Here there are more oak doors set into the exposed granite walls. The first door on the left gives access to the public bar which has two large oak beams supporting the main section of the ceiling. The second door on the left leads into the snug bar. On the right of the corridor is the residents' lounge and at the end, also on the right, is the dining room which was formerly a kitchen.

The double doors on the left of the inn used to give access to the yard and stables at the rear, which would have seen much use during the years when the turnpike road from Okehampton to Exeter passed through South Zeal and the inn was a well known coaching inn. The yard has since been concreted over and the stables converted into a bungalow. It has been rumoured that there are two tunnels hidden beneath the inn, one leading to Oxenham Manor at South Tawton and the other surfacing somewhere on the moor nearby.

Charles Kingsley was one of three famous west country authors to have incorporated the inn in their books, Eden Phillpotts and the Reverend Sabine Baring-Gould being the others. Charles Kingsley in his book *Westward Ho* tells of the tragic events which befell the Oxenham family between 1618-1773 following an appearance by a white bird. It was said that after a sighting of this bird, one of the members of the family was sure to die within days. Lady Margaret Oxenham was visited by this bird on the eve of her wedding, although she did not actually see it. Her father saw it but did not say anything, maybe things would have ended differently if he had, as Lady Margaret was stabbed to death by a jealous lover as she stood at the altar of the church at South Tawton on her wedding day.

In the 18th century William Oxenham also received a visit from the white bird as he lay sick in bed. Even though he knew of the legend he scoffed at it, saying that he did not feel sick enough to die. A few days later death caught up with him. The last member of the Oxenham family died in Canada earlier this century, but there was no sighting of the bird as far as is known.

44: Packhorse Hotel

In Plymouth Road, South Brent.
Tel: South Brent (0364) 72283

The Packhorse Hotel dates from the beginning of the 17th century. It was a former packhorse station on the old Plymouth to London turnpike road. The inn is built on land that until the reign of King Henry VIII, belonged to Buckfast Abbey. With the dissolution of the monasteries, the land passed into the hands of the Petre family. The stables were situated at the rear of the building but these were unfortunately destroyed by vandals in 1975. The old forge, where the blacksmith shod many a horse, is now the kitchen. In the 1700s the rent was £20 a year, in those days quite expensive.

The public bar has a large open fireplace set into a section of exposed-stone wall. The walls in the family room, which also has a large fireplace, has some antique mirrors advertising different brands of spirits on them.

Family Orders punctually attended to.

Bass' and Allsopp's Pale Ales.

WM. EDDLES,
Wine and Spirit Merchant,

AND AGENT FOR WORTHINGTON & CO'S BURTON ALES, &C.,

"CROWN HOTEL,"

ST. MARY CHURCH,

T O R Q U A Y.

45: Palk Arms

In the Village of Hennock, 2.5 miles from Chudleigh Knighton.
Tel: Hennock (0626) 833027.

The Palk Arms is thought to date from the 16th century and was one of two inns in the village. The name was taken from the Palk family who owned a vast amount of land in the surrounding area. Next door to the Palk Arms which sold mostly ale, was the Union Inn which sold mostly cider.

In the early years of this century the inns would open from 6am until

10pm at night. The Union Inn finally closed its doors in the late 1950s.

The interior of the Palk Arms was altered in 1979 after the lower level had been partially destroyed by fire. The walls separating the original smaller public bar from the landlord's sitting room, and the wall dividing the lounge bar from the family room were removed, forming the through-lounge bar and family room seen today. The public bar has a large open exposed-stone fireplace and, hanging from the granite walls, are some old animal traps. The restaurant, which has extensive views of the Teign Valley, including Trusham, Chudleigh and Chudleigh Knighton, was added in 1990 and is built on top of the old stables, now converted into a kitchen. Set into a wall in the ladies toilet is a baker's oven, still in a remarkable condition.

46: Peter Tavy Inn

Situated in the old mining village of Peter Tavy near Tavistock.
Tel: Mary Tavy (082281 348)

The Peter Tavy Inn, dating from 15th century, developed from a farm cottage and blacksmith's shop. The latter is now the serving bar and in one corner of it, in the ceiling, there used to be a trap door leading to the bedroom above. The children of a former landlord had to use this entrance to their bedroom when the everyday entrance was barred to them while the Royal Order of Buffaloes were holding one of their meetings in the main upstairs room. After their meetings members of the Order would come downstairs, walk out of the inn and enter the recent extension to the bar via an outside door, ordering their drinks through a small hatchway in the dividing wall. This wall has since been removed, giving access to the room through the bar.

Frank 'Axeman' Mitchell, who was the only man to escape from Princetown Prison without recapture, is reputed to have enjoyed the hospitality of the inn, his bills being paid by one of the notorious Kray Twins. The cheque was said to have been attached to one of the wooden ceiling beams behind the bar for a while.

There is a rather amusing story attached to the inn involving an earlier landlord, a former vicar of the nearby church, and the church warden who had happened to be a relative of the landlord. The vicar would not start his sermon during the Sunday service whilst there was anyone drinking at the inn, and he would send his church warden to make sure the inn was empty. This caused the church warden some concern as he did not want to upset his cousin, so on his way he would walk slowly, looking down at his feet, saying rather loudly 'I am coming, cousin Tom, I am coming cousin Tom'. On his arrival he would find the bar empty (everybody having had time to hide in another room). He would then return to the vicar and report with all honesty that the bar was empty!

47: Plume of Feathers

In the centre of Princetown on the B3212 Two Bridges-Yelverton Road.
Tel: (082289) 240

Built in 1785, during the reign of King George III, the Plume of Feathers was the first substantial building in Princetown, originally accommodating the men working on the country home of Sir Thomas Tyrwhitt at nearby Tor Royal.

The exterior of the building has changed very little since then, although during the last twenty years there have been many changes made inside. The original kitchen was made into today's top bar, and the outhouse, where the ducks and chickens were kept, was converted into a kitchen. A new kitchen was opened early in 1991, occupying part of what was the old gift shop. It was also at this time that the Alpine Bunkhouse was built onto the main building at the rear. The hostel accommodation used to be the shippens.

The public bar, with its beamed ceiling, used to be the snug bar, separated from the other rooms of the inn by wooden dividing walls, the main staircase went up through the ceiling in this room, near to the corner of the bar.

Over the years there has been more than one strange occurrence at the inn, and it has jokingly been referred to as the 'Plume of Doom'. Ladies be warned, you might feel an icy presence while you make use of the ladies toilets at the eastern end of the inn.

This ghostly presence has been felt many times without there ever being a sighting. On more than one occasion, guests staying the night in the room on the middle floor have complained that they have felt someone trying to pull the bedclothes from their beds during the night. Others staying at the inn have said that they have heard the sound of a mother crying over the death of her young child.

48: Plymouth Inn

In Court Street, Moretonhampstead, 14 miles from Exeter.
Tel: Moretonhampstead (0647) 40266

The 17th century Plymouth Inn is a double-fronted building with bow windows on either side of the main door. It wasn't until 1835 that the first record of it being an inn appeared. Its name is taken from the Exeter-Moretonhampstead-Plymouth road alongside which it is sited.

In its early days it was a bustling coaching inn and the garden area at the rear was where the stables were situated. These were reached by travelling along the covered alleyway, now concealed by large double doors. The old horse-tethering hooks can still be seen along the rear exterior wall of the building.

The inn consists of two adjoining bar areas separated by an archway in an exposed granite wall. Along the alleyway is a door that now leads into the public bar, but which used to give access to the 'bottle and jug' at the far end of a narrow passage.

Unlike many of the public houses in Moretonhampstead, the Plymouth Inn appears to have emerged unscathed from the many disastrous fires that swept through the town in the 19th century.

49: Post Inn

Beside the A30 at Whiddon Down, 7 miles from Okehampton.
Tel: Whiddon Down (064723) 242

The Post Inn, formerly the Post Office Inn once formed part of a chain of roadside inns upon which the history of the Post Office was founded. This inn is thought to have been built in the 16th century, after Henry VIII had started a network for mail to be delivered around the country. In 1516 a series of posting houses was set-up where the king's courier could get fresh horses. Obvious choices were the roadside inns.

In 1635 The Royal Post Service was thrown open for public use with the innkeepers also serving as postmasters. During the 1650s in Oliver Cromwell's rule, these innkeepers/postmasters were virtually government spies, the innkeeper at the Post Inn helping to keep an eye on the travellers on the turnpike road from Cornwall. In 1784 the first mail coach service was introduced, with fresh horses provided at approximately ten mile intervals. A few years later post office policy changed and mail was switched away from the inns. The job went instead to local traders, or even the schoolmaster, until Post Offices opened.

On the 22 January 1964 the name of the inn was changed to the Post Inn. The building has expanded over the years with the acquisition of the adjoining cottages, part of which now form the public bar at one end, and dining room at the other. The original building now houses the lounge bar and a section of the dining room. The ceiling is decorated with a large collection of horse brasses adorning the wooden beams and the wood-framed partition section of the wall. When landlord John Youldon first took over the inn in 1987 there were only thirty pieces of brassware, now grown to more than 750.

There is no stopping some people's desire to get to their local, as two regulars proved when the front of the building was completely covered with deep snow during the blizzard of 1963. They tunnelled from the main road to the entrance door, thus gaining entry. I wonder if they received a free pint for their efforts?

50: Prewley Moor Arms

Just off the roundabout at Sourton Cross, 2 miles from Okehampton.
Tel: Bridestowe (083786) 349

The Prewley Moor Arms is Dartmoor's newest inn, having opened its doors to the public on 13 May 1989. The licence was granted in 1988, prior to the completion of work on the inn. The building is made from two 16th century cottages combined to make one larger cottage.

This was the home of Tom and Joyce Honey before they acquired the cottage and adjacent camp site. They then had the idea to turn it into an inn, which they designed and built. The interior comprises a large open-plan public bar with an oak-beamed ceiling and exposed stone fireplaces at either end. The smaller fireplace is an original.

There has been an inn at Sourton Crossroads for at least two hundred years. In the field adjoining the inn, there used to be a barn that was formerly an ale house, dating from the early 19th century. Unfortunately when the road was widened the barn was demolished.

51: Prince of Wales

Approximately 200 yards along the B3357 Princetown-Rundlestone Road
from The Duchy Hotel, Princetown. Tel: Princetown (082289) 219

The Prince of Wales was built in 1854 (the third public house to be built in
Princetown) and was sold to the first owner for £400. The exterior of the
inn has changed very little over the years, although the interior has seen
some changes. The restaurant, added in 1989, was formerly part of the
backyard which was then covered with a roof and later enclosed to make a
bottle store. The public bar has exposed stone walls complete with three
large stone fireplaces. An assortment of wind chimes can be found hanging
from various parts of the beamed ceiling.

There is a striking difference between the Prince of Wales and nearby

buildings - in stark contrast to the cold grey granite seen all around in Princetown, the exterior has been painted in a pastel colour, changed annually by the landlord (in 1990 it was pink).

If, for any reason, you were to be in the public bar during the early hours of the morning, you might share the experience of one resident as he sat chatting to the landlord who was tidying-up from the evening before. A ghostly figure dressed in priest's robes was seen drifting across the room. The startled resident almost had a heart attack and dashed out the rear door. The landlord showed no surprise at all because he had seen this eerie figure on numerous occasions. Could this be the unsettled spirit of a previous landlord who committed suicide on the premises 25 years ago?

52: Red Lion

East Street, Ashburton.
Tel: Ashburton (0364) 52378

The Red Lion was built in the 18th century and was formerly connected to the Golden Lion. The original, much smaller inn, consisted of just the two rooms at the front, that on the left being the landlord's living quarters, with the bar on the right side. These have since been converted into the small lounge bar and part of the larger public bar. Where the electricity sub-station is now situated was a small inn called the 'Tap', and in the days of travel by horse-drawn coaches it was a popular place for coachmen to stay. They would lead their horses through the Red Lion and stable them in what is now the Red Lion's beer cellar.

There is supposedly a poltergeist haunting this inn but its identity is a

mystery. Pictures have been thrown many feet from the walls into the centre of the rooms but no one has been seen to do this.

The Red Lion has, since 1944, run club outings annually by coach to various parts of the South West. This is thought to be the longest continuous run of its kind, in Great Britain. The walls of the public bar have a display of photographs showing many of the people who have been on these trips over the years.

53: Ring O' Bells

At Chagford Square, 3 miles from the A30 at Whiddon Down
and 2.5 miles from Moretonhampstead. Tel: Chagford (0647) 432466

The Ring O' Bells dates from the 16th century, being an ale house tied to the church, although there is thought to have been an inn on this site since 1177 providing shelter for pilgrims who visited an old Christian shrine in the vicinity (long before the church was built). There are records that show that ale was supplied to the church by the Ring O' Bells well into the 19th century. The bell ringers were regular receivers of ale following practice ringing, marriages and on any other public occasion. They would come over to the inn for their ale which was charged to church funds. The inn was rebuilt in 1861 after it had been completely destroyed by fire in 1860.

The plain white front of the building hides behind it an interesting olde worlde inn that has, over the years served more than one purpose. The 'Stannary Buttery' was once used as a holding prison for prisoners being taken to the assizes at Okehampton. During the 16th century the room at the front upstairs was used as a Stannary Court room. Chagford became a Stannary Town in 1305, as were Tavistock, Plympton and Ashburton; it was at these towns that tin mined in Devon would be weighed and stamped. The Stannary Courts had the power to send any law-breaker to be held in the notorious Lydford Castle.

There was also a court held here when required by the Crownery Court. This was used whenever a sudden death occurred in the parish and the

Crowner, who was fetched from Black Torrington, and twelve jurymen would determine if it had been a suicide or not. If it had been a suicide, the body would be buried at a crossroad outside the Parish; the ceremony being carried-out at night, without prayer!

The room at the back, upstairs, was at one time used as a mortuary. Also at the rear of the inn, there used to be (between the years 1889-1930), a butcher's shop in what was a converted old barn; this has since been demolished.

In 1976 the Inn was completely refurbished with wood panelling covering the walls of the main bar helping to retain an olde worlde atmosphere. Unfortunately, the large open fireplace in this room no longer burns wood or coal due to the fact that even on a still day with no wind, smoke would blow back into the room. The fireplace in the 'Stannary Buttery' (which had been covered up and substituted with an electric fire for many years) has once again been restored to its former glory.

Hanging above the Bar is a collection of ten cow bells, each a different size - a 'ring' of bells that were given by a customer who thought that the inn should live up to its name.

Since the beginning of 1990 when the inn was re-wired and plumbed, a series of unaccountable happenings have taken place. There has been loud banging heard from the cellar when nobody was there; pictures hanging on the thick walls have been thrown many feet into the middle of the floor. Could the spirits of those who had rested awhile in the mortuary be complaining about the alterations made to the building during recent years?

Chagford, The Square

54: Ring of Bells

Just off the Village Green, North Bovey.
2 miles from Moretonhampstead. Tel: (0647) 40375

The Ring of Bells, which was built in the mid 13th century, has changed very little over the years. The main building with its thatched roof, thick granite walls and low ceilings, was built originally as a lodging house for the stonemasons who were building the nearby church of St John the Baptist. A little later on it became a farmhouse and the date when it first became an inn is uncertain. It was most probably an ale house for the stonemasons, and then farmworkers, early in its history. The extension housing the dining room was added in the 15th century.

The stables, where over the years many fine steeplechasers were bred, was converted in 1967 by John Brackenbury into today's Stable Bar. The

old cobbled stone floor still remains. The bar originally stood along the far wall.

The narrow space between the main building and the stables (where the hay carts were stored), locally known as the cart linhay, has been incorporated into part of the bar. Skittles was also played here, the players rolling the balls from outside at the pins placed in the linhay. The windows nearby still have the iron bars covering them which were used to protect them from any wayward balls.

One of the inn's most famous guests was the world-famous country singer Dolly Parton who stayed overnight whilst on a private visit to Devon.

55: Rising Sun

Beside the A30, 0.5 mile from South Zeal, and 4 miles from
Okehampton. Tel: Okehampton (0837) 840215

The date when the Rising Sun was built is uncertain, but it is thought to
have been in the 16th century and as far as is known has always been an
inn. It has thick cob walls and comprises a lounge, dining room, public bar
with a high oak-beamed ceiling, and children's room. Originally the
entrance door used to be in the front of the building, this opened into a
passageway which separated a smaller public bar from the ladies room and
led up to the wide staircase. The dividing walls were removed in the early
1940s to make the large public bar seen today. The children's room was
formerly the kitchen and in here, set into a recess, is a stone fireplace built
on a raised section of the floor. There is also a blocked-off doorway which
gave access to the scullery and dairy situated at the side and rear of the

building. There are still a few locals that frequent the inn who can remember coming here when they were young to purchase milk and eggs.

Underneath the building there used to be a boiler room and, in the years after the Second World War, the responsibility for lighting the boiler fell to Ted Hill, a local man from South Zeal. Ted was the only person able to get the boiler burning and his services were used by three successive landlords. Many a walker coming off the moor in the pouring rain has dried their clothes by the heat from the boiler.

Many years ago the coalman from North Tawton used to pass here with his horse and cart on his way to Okehampton to collect his supply of coal. On the return journey he always stopped off here for a quick pint. One day though he was taken ill and a replacement made the journey instead, without his knowing way, the horse stopped as usual outside on the return journey. Try as he might he could not get the horse to move. Seeing what was happening the landlord went out and told the coalman that if he would just walk inside the inn and out again the horse was sure to continue with the journey.

56: Rock Inn

In Haytor Vale, not far from Haytor Rocks.
Tel: Haytor (03646) 305

The Rock Inn, formerly a coaching inn and then hotel, was built, along with the surrounding cottages, at the instigation of George Templer around the year 1826. The cottages were to house the quarrymen working in Templer's quarry at nearby Haytor, and the purpose-built inn to provide a place of sustenance and relaxation. All the buildings are constructed from local granite. The original inglenook fireplace in the bar of the inn has a log fire which burns all year round and is said never to go out.

There has been a sighting, late at night, of a woman dressed in grey, sweeping the floors on the upper level of the inn. When approached she

suddenly disappears into thin air. This is Belinda, the inn's hard-working ghost. Belinda, a serving wench at the inn just over a hundred years ago, had an affair with a local coachman. Unfortunately for her his wife found out and murdered her one evening on the back stairs of the inn.

Reproduced with permission of Elizabeth Stanbrook.

57: Rock Inn

Just off the roundabout at Yelverton, 9 miles from Plymouth.
Tel: Yelverton (0822) 852022

The Rock Inn is one of the oldest buildings in Yelverton. Records show it to have been in existence in 1828 as a dwelling-house known as the Rock House. It is thought originally it was a farmhouse dating from the 15th century and the structure of the nearby stables has been estimated to date from that period.

Records of 1862 show William Shillabeer, Victualler, Rock Hotel, but how long before that it became an hotel is uncertain. For a while, it was known as the Blatchford Rock Hotel. The hotel had been developed with the acquisition of the old stables from Sir Massey Lopes by the Shillabeer Sisters, who in 1905 were joined by Algy Langton, their nephew. In 1966 the hotel closed and parts of it were made into flats. The bars that occupied the main section of the premises remained and became the Rock Inn.

58: Royal Standard

On the A386 Okehampton-Tavistock Road at Mary Tavy
Tel: Mary Tavy (082281) 289

This inn, which has retained all of its original character including its beamed ceilings, is approximately 300 years old. It started as the end cottage in a row of miners' cottages. Two of the miners from the nearby Wheal Betsy silver, lead, copper and arsenic mine turned it into a beer house, with a single bar, selling ale from a couple of beer barrels in the corner of the room. Their main customers were local farmers and other miners. The long-disused horse-drawn railway running from the mine to Mary Tavy station passed behind the cottages.

Around the turn of the century the middle section of the bar was built along the length of the building with the final section being added eleven years ago. The main window of the bar was of frosted glass and displayed the sign of the Octagon Brewery from Plymouth.

It is reputed that the inn has played host to royal patronage when a young prince stayed for one night during the last century. This allowed the landlord at that time to change the name from the original Blackdown Inn to its present name of Royal Standard. The royal standard is displayed on the sign outside, an honour granted only by royal permission.

Charles II and the Royal Oak

Two years after King Charles I had been executed, his son Charles II was defeated by Parliamentarian troops on 3 September 1651 at the Battle of Worcester. For six weeks following Charles became a hunted fugitive before escaping from Shoreham on 15 October 1651 to safety in France. He had travelled over 400 miles throughout England seeking shelter, often staying at wayside inns and assuming many different disguises.

On 6 September 1651 at Boscoble in Staffordshire, he and another fugitive, Major Careless, hid in an oak tree from morning until dusk. The original tree has since disappared. The tree now at Boscoble grew from an acorn from the original. After the restoration of the monarchy Charles's adventure was recorded on many inn signs. There are about 800 Royal Oak inns throughout England, four of them being within Dartmoor National Park.

59: Royal Oak

East Street, Ashburton.
Tel: Ashburton (0364) 52444

The Royal Oak dates back to the 14th or 15th centuries and has been an inn for at least 300 years. It was formerly a busy travellers' tavern on the old turnpike road between Plymouth and Exeter. The inn has been enlarged over the years with the acquisition of the buildings at the rear. The exterior walls of those buildings have since revealed several old fireplaces dating from medieval times, the one in the rear wall being a fine example. In June 1990, when the inn was undergoing alterations to the roof, builders discovered a series of medieval arch-braced roof trusses. The complete roof has survived. They also unearthed many interesting items, including old clay pipes, buttons from military uniforms, musket balls dating from 1640, and various coins, the earliest being from the 18th century. In 1646, during the Civil

War, General Fairfax and his troops were billeted at Ashburton before engaging in the Battle of Heathfield. The General stayed at The Mermaid Inn, now 'A R Church' (Ironmongers) in North Street, whilst some of his troops were billeted at The Royal Oak.

The inn has an oak-beamed public bar and restaurant, and the end wall in the bar is of exposed stone and has an open stone fireplace. Until the flood-prevention work was carried out in the town, the ground floor of the inn was sometimes flooded to a depth of up to three feet, as water flowed in a torrent down East and West Streets during heavy rains. Unfortunately the Royal Oak was situated at the lowest point in the centre of the town.

60: Royal Oak

In the Village of Dunsford, 7 miles from Exeter.
Tel: Christow (0647) 52256

It is believed that the Royal Oak was built in the 15th century, housing the stonemasons working on the nearby church of St. Mary. The inn was part of

Fulford Estate, as was most of Dunsford at one time; Sir Francis Fulford was a staunch Royalist supporter and it was he who gave the inn its name.

The original inn, which had thick cob walls and a thatched roof, was destroyed by fire in 1887, reputedly on the same night that the Theatre Royal in Exeter was burnt down (with the loss of 186 lives).

The inn was rebuilt shortly after and remained part of the Fulford Estate until 1954 when it was sold to St Anne's Brewery. The inn is built on a split level, comprising a lounge bar, with an exposed stone fireplace, public bar and dining room on the upper level. On the lower level is the games room. At the rear of the building are situated five en-suite rooms that have been converted from an old barn and stables. At one time, and up to 1960, the inn was combined with a farm. The two cottages adjoining the inn's car park were once the cow shed with a hayloft above.

61: Royal Oak Inn

1.5 miles from Yelverton, and the Plymouth to Tavistock road,
12 miles from Plymouth. Tel: Yelverton 852944

It is uncertain when the inn was first built, the most popular theory is that it was built in the 15th Century, but there is reason to believe that it might have been built in 1122, at the same time as the nearby church of St Peter. There is a receipt for 2s.6d in the Plymouth Records Office for wine and ale paid for by a man working on Drake's Leat, dated 1589, so we know that the inn has been selling ale for at least 400 years.

The Royal Oak, which is built of stone and cob, started out as a church house and was used as a resting place by monks travelling between the abbeys of Tavistock and Buckfast. It would also have been a popular place for people who had walked many miles across the moor to the church on a Sunday, and needed to refresh themselves before their return journey.

The inn was named, according to records, after the oak tree nearby, which is thought to have been planted in the reign of King John. The trunk of the tree has been hollow for at least a hundred years, and was once used to store peat.

The building is now owned by the parish council, being one of only two in England so owned. The inn was purchased from the church in the early 19th Century. The landlord is a tenant and pays rent to the council.

There are two bars. The public bar, or local's bar, has a slate floor, open log fire and side seats. The spacious lounge bar, with its beamed ceiling and thick walls, retains the charm of an old Dartmoor inn.

62: Royal Oak

In Station Road, South Brent.
Tel: South Brent (0364) 72133

The Royal Oak was built in the early 19th century under a cloud of animosity and revenge. There were certain religious factions that did not want any public houses in South Brent. They bought the Clarence Inn, then sited opposite the present position of the London Inn, and promptly closed it down. The London Inn was then built to replace it. The people who had bought and closed the Clarence Inn, then bought and promptly closed the original Royal Oak Inn, now the cottage that is next door to the Royal Oak Hotel. The Hotel was built by the same people who had built The London Inn.

Over the years this inn has on occasions served a dual purpose. The public bar, which has thick pillars supporting massive beams, has been used as a court room; the Judge's chair can be seen near the fireplace.

On the 1 July 1911, Mr A. Catt, the landlord, was awarded a contract to carry the Post Office mail to Kingsbridge and the inn then became a busy post house. The mail, which had arrived by railway and horse-drawn coaches was sorted here. The stables, where spare horses were kept, were situated opposite the inn and were converted in the 1970s into two modern houses.

The Beer Cellar is underground and is partially cooled by a stream which used to run directly through the middle of the cellar, but is now piped just below. There is an interesting public notice, close to where the stream used to exit from the building, which reads as follows:

PUBLIC HEALTH ACTS - CAUTION

Notice is hereby given that any person washing carts, entrails or offensive matter in this stream, or otherwise fouling the same are liable to be convicted by a Court of Summary Jurisdiction under the above acts and will be proceeded against.

The Totnes Rural District Council.

By Order   *Thos Windeatt*

63: The Rugglestone Inn

In the Village of Widecombe-In-The-Moor on the road from the church to Venton.

At first glance, as you drive past, you might mistake the building for a typically beautiful Dartmoor cottage. It is not until you notice the words 'Rugglestone Inn' on the sign below the roof that you realise its true identity.

The building serves a dual purpose, mainly being the home of the landlady, and secondly an inn. The serving bar at the rear of the building is reached by the narrow passageway leading from the main door, and the bar room or lounge is on the right.

The Inn is named after the enormous logan stone, to be found not far from the rear of the inn. This stone measures approximately 22ft long, 16ft wide and has 4 sides measuring in depth, respectively 20ft, 19ft, 16ft and

12.5 ft. The weight of this stone is estimated to be 115 tons. This enormous rock rests on the supporting rocks below and it is said that it could be made to rock with the aid of the key of the nearby church.

64: Sandypark Inn

2.5 miles from Whiddon Down and Chagford on the A382.
Tel: Moretonhampstead (0647) 433538

The best way to describe this inn is to say that it is exactly what you would expect from your 'local'. It has a relaxed and comfortable feeling. The building, with its thatched roof and thick granite walls, dates back to the 16th century, and is thought to have always been an inn, starting as a coaching house on the old turnpike road between Okehampton and Moretonhampstead. Opposite the inn was a barn and blacksmith's shop, converted some years ago into the cottages seen today.

The inn comprises a public bar, which has been created from three small rooms. It has a low oak-beamed ceiling and uncovered concrete floor. There are wooden bench seats, and pine panelling surrounds the lower half of the walls. There is a lounge bar which serves as a dining room, and sited behind the public bar is a smaller room, now commonly known as the snug bar.

65: Seven Stars

In the Village of South Tawton.
Tel: Okehampton (0837) 840229

There has been an inn on this site since the 17th century, although the Seven Stars was built at the end of the 19th century, replacing the previous inn which was detroyed by fire.

Originally the Seven Stars belonged to Colonel Letheridge and was part of the Wood Estate. The exterior of the building has changed very little since it was erected, the only change being the removal of the porch above the front door due to the weakening of its supports. The large public bar was once three smaller rooms, one of which was used by the Colonel himself. The oak beams supporting the ceiling were brought over from the nearby Oxenham Manor.

Until 1989 the Seven Stars was partially within the Dartmoor National Park, the stable bar, which was formerly the old stables, used to be outside the boundary line.

66: Skylark Inn

In the Hamlet of Clearbook, 1 mile from the A386 Plymouth to Yelverton road. Tel: (0822) 853258

The Skylark Inn is thought to have been built in the early 18th century, the first record of it being in 1780 when it was just an isolated farmhouse. It was ten years later, in 1790, that it became an ale house for the miners, working at the nearby Yeoland tin mine. Over the years there have been many alterations to the building, both inside and out. The original front

doorway had two doors, one opened into the public bar and the other into the private bar which had softer seats, but you paid a little more for your ale.

The changes to the interior were made in 1950 when the two bars and the original slate-floored kitchen (situated where the main bar now is) were all knocked into one. The wooden beams on the ceiling now display a collection of brassware from horse harnesses. Built into one wall of the public bar there is a large baker's oven which protrudes out into the cellar on the opposite side. This oven might have had limited usage before the bakery was opened behind the Post Office.

Where the car park now is, there once was a substantial open-fronted shed, at the rear of which was a courtyard where customers could leave their horses and carts while they went inside for a drink. On one occasion, while one customer was having a few too many glasses of ale, his pals decided to play a prank on him. They went out to the yard and unhitched his horse from the cart. They then pushed the shafts of the cart through the gate before harnessing the horse up again.

Photograph reproduced with permission of the landlord

67: Sun Inn

In Church Street, Buckfastleigh.
Tel: Buckfastleigh (0364) 42397

The date when the Sun Inn was first built is uncertain, although it is thought that it has been an inn for about a hundred years. The inn was bought by Heavitree Brewery for £2500 in 1929 from Edwin Tucker and Sons, maltsters from Newton Abbot. The interior has altered very little since then and comprises a small lounge bar, games room and public bar that has a small exposed-stone fireplace.

Many years ago farmers from the locality would hold regular meetings here. They would leave their horses in the stables situated at the rear of the building.

There is thought to be a ghost frequenting the tiny room in the loft space, No one has seen it though, but noises have been heard that cannot be accounted for and taps on gas bottles in the cellar have unaccountably been turned off.

68: Tavistock Inn

Beside the Ashburton-Two Bridges Road at Poundsgate.
Tel: Poundsgate (03643) 251

The Tavistock Inn was probably built in the 14th century and is thought to have been a farmhouse before it became an inn.

It started out as a single roomed building, with an outside staircase leading to a large one-roomed bedroom where weary travellers could lay their bed rolls for a small charge. The staircase was added in the 15th century. There is a small alcove near the top of this staircase which was at

first thought to be a niche where a candle could be placed. Because of the presence of a wooden lintel this idea was dismissed and the alcove was more likely to be a small outside window. About a hundred years after the outside staircase was added the ends and back of the building were extended.

There is a handsome fireplace in the bar, which is very pleasant to sit beside on a cold wintery day. Many years ago a large oven was found in the fireplace. Here was baked the bread for the village. In the building records in Exeter, it states that there are two ovens but the whereabouts of the second is still unknown, most probably bricked-up somewhere in the fireplace.

Tavistock Inn 1896 reproduced with permission of Mrs. Comer

Originally the inn was a part of the Spitchwick Estate. A hundred year lease had been created by Lord Ashburton, who was the freeholder at the time. When the lease expired there was no direct line of descent and when the inn was put up for sale it took a Court at Chancery twenty years to determine who was the legal claimant. It is said that claimants were coming out of the woodwork. When the legal title was finally resolved the inn was sold in 1860 to the tenant at the time for £114.

After complaints from customers about the dust which fell from the worm-eaten beams, the ceiling was completely replaced in 1939. The old beams were offered to the landlady for firewood, but she was unable to cut them as the wood was still as hard as iron.

There is a well known story about the devil calling at the inn on the afternoon of 21 October 1638 on his way to Widecombe-in-the-Moor (the day of the terrible thunderstorm when the church tower was struck by lightning and four people killed). He bought a pint of ale which sizzled as it went down his throat and on placing the empty tankard on the bar it scorched a mark which was there for all to see until about twelve years ago, when the present bar was installed. He then paid the landlady with coins that turned to dry leaves and blew away as soon as he left.

There is another amusing story concerning the landlady whose hunter mare was in season and had attracted the unwanted attentions of a Dartmoor pony stallion. This stallion had been shoo'd away many times, but on one occasion at about 3 o'clock in the morning the landlady was awakened by a terrible noise coming from the area of the stables. When she went down to investigate, still clad in her nightclothes, she found the Dartmoor stallion attempting to get into the stables. She then proceeded to chase the pony down the main road with a broom in her hand!

69: Teignhouse Inn

Six miles from Exeter beside the B3193 at the Junction of the road to Doddiscombsleigh. Tel: Christow (0647) 52286

The Teignhouse Inn was built originally as a farmhouse in the 18th century. The date when it first became an inn is uncertain although it states in White's Directory for 1850 that there was a Teign House Inn in existence at that time. It most probably started selling ale and cider to the farm workers and miners working in the locality before becoming solely an inn. With the increased traffic along the B3193, following the opening of the Great Western Railways 'Teign Valley Line' in 1882, and subsequent building of the nearby Christow railway station, the Teign House Inn found itself in the centre of a busy area. There used to be a cattle and produce market held every first Monday in the month at the rear of the inn and the meadow in front was used as a race track for horses.

70: Three Crowns Hotel

In the centre of Chagford opposite the Church of St. Michael, 5 miles from Whiddon Down.Tel: Chagford (06473) 3444

The Three Crowns Hotel is a beautiful building with thick granite walls and fine mullion windows. It was originally built as a manor house by John Whyddon incorporating parts of a 13th century monks' hospice. It later became a church house, being owned and maintained by the church. Later still it became the dower house of the Whiddon family, being part of Whiddon Park estate.

The date when it first became an inn is uncertain. The first recorded name it had is The Black Swan. The name coming from the black swan which was added to the family crest of Judge Whyddon by Queen Mary for his services as judge in the notorious case of Thomas Stafford, who had rebelled against the Queen. The trial was so dangerous that the judge tried the case dressed in armour.

In the early 17th century the building witnessed two tragedies, the first being in 1641 when Mary Whyddon was shot by a jealous lover at the entrance of the building as she returned from her wedding in the nearby church of St Michael. The second tragedy came in February 1643 when Sidney Godolphin, a young cavalry officer, also a poet and Member of Parliament for Helston, was shot following the battle at Bloody Meadow near the head of Fingle Gorge. He was taken to the Three Crowns and laid on a stone bench in the porch before being taken to the Tower Room where he died from his wounds. He was buried in Okehampton on the 10 February 1643. His ghost has been heard occasionally pacing the corridors of the inn. The Godolphin Bar has been named in his memory.

Reproduced with permission of the landlord

The Hotel now comprises a spacious dining room and the Godolphin and Whyddon lounge Bar. Both bars have open fireplaces of exposed stone. The one in the Whyddon Bar has three large brass crowns attached to the beam across the top of it. The huge oak beams supporting the ceilings are remarkably well preserved.

71: The Tors

In the Old Saxon Village of Belstone, 3 miles from Okehampton.

Tel: Okehampton (0837) 840689

The Tors Hotel was built at the end of the 19th century and replaced the Old Inn that was destroyed by fire in 1896. It was intended that the house built on the lower edge of the village green would be the inn and the

interior was fitted-out with a serving hatch which has survived to this day. The magistrates at Okehampton refused to grant a licence for this building and the inn was subsequently built on its present site backing on to the graveyard of the church of St Mary. It's a great pity that the inn was not allowed to be where first intended, just think of the beautiful view, with the village green and the great dome of Cosdon before you.

The inn was built by local stonemasons from granite brought from the tors nearby. Originally there were two public bars and, running along where the bar is now situated, was a long corridor. The interior underwent a complete refurbishment in 1973.

The Old Inn
From a drawing by Miss Margaret James

Not many years after the inn was built the landlord found himself in a spot of trouble with the law when he allowed a bit of after-hours drinking to take place. The local policeman, noting that the lights were still on and hearing loud sounds of merriment, knocked on the front door. After the door was opened and he had entered the passageway, he was asked by the landlord to remove his helmet. On his arrival into the public bar he took the particulars of everyone he found drinking. When the case came before the magistrates the solicitor for the defendant successfully argued their case, stating that as the constable was not wearing his helmet at the time he was not correctly dressed, and because of this the magistrates dismissed the case.

72: Tradesmans Arms

In the Village of Scorriton, 2.5 miles from Buckfastleigh and 0.5 mile from Holne. Tel: Poundsgate (03643) 206

The Tradesmans Arms is thought to be between two and three hundred years old. It is not certain if it has always been an inn although at the beginning of the 19th century it would have seen much use by the miners working at the nearby mines of Henroost, Hooten Wheals and Hexworthy. The track from that area of the moor, via Chalk Ford to Buckfastleigh, passed close by the inn.

The interior comprises of the main bar, family room and snug bar. The main bar was refurbished in 1986. The snug bar was constructed at the beginning of this century and was first used as the village shop. This remained in business until 1968 when it finally ceased trading. This room, with its cloth-covered bench seats is secluded from the rest of the inn giving a touch of intimacy. Don't be fooled by the face looking down from the beam in the snug. It's not made from wood, as one visitor once loudly boasted to his companion, it's made from ordinary plaster, stained to match the wood.

73: Two Bridges Hotel

On the B3357 at Two Bridges, 1.5 miles from Princetown.
Tel: Princetown (082289) 206

The exact date of the building of the Two Bridges Hotel is uncertain. Records show that in 1805 Sir Francis Buller and others took out a ninety-nine year lease on the Saracen's Head inn, as the hotel was then called, although the inn had already been in existence long before that date.

It is thought that the inn originated in 1767 as an ale house when there used to be a market here between potato traders from various parts of the moor. The name of the Saracen's Head was taken from part of Sir Francis Buller's family crest.

Reproduced from a watercolour by John Swete

In 1866 the inn was almost completely destroyed by fire with only the outer walls remaining. The position was considered as a possible site for the Duchy Office on Dartmoor. However, the inn was rebuilt. A few years later when it became an important posting inn, a blacksmith's shop became a necessity and one of the out-buildings was converted for this purpose.

The lease of the inn was put up for auction in 1855 and Mrs W. Smith, the inn's tenant, bought it. She did not own it for very long and, in 1893, the inn came into the hands of Mr Trinaman who was an exceptional businessman, and he was instrumental in many changes taking place. During his first year he had water piped to the inn and had bathrooms and other conveniences fitted. It was also at this time that a greater interest was being shown by the Victorians in the nature and wilderness of the moor and, being ideally situated in the heart of Dartmoor, business improved considerably. It was in 1893 that the name of the inn was changed to its present name.

In 1905 the building was greatly improved when new chimneys were added, the walls mortared, and new doors fitted inside and out. The work was carried-out by John Halfyard from Princetown. Five years later further work was undertaken when the hotel was enlarged and the timber framed section of the building was replaced by stone.

74: Union Inn

In Ford Street, Moretonhampstead, 5 miles from the A30 at Whiddon Down, 14 miles from Exeter. Tel: Moretonhampstead (0647) 40397

Originally named The Swan Inn, the 17th century Union Inn was formerly the property of the church and was the responsibility of the churchwardens. The inn was granted its first licence after being recommended by the church minister and churchwardens. In 1807 the name of the inn was changed to its present name. The inn's sign is hand-carved and shows two clasped hands. The building was originally thatched but unfortunately, due to the weight of the thatch and the deterioration of the beams, which were old tree trunks, the roof collapsed in 1966 and was replaced with slate.

The public bar used to be a men-only bar, with women being allowed to use only the smaller room at the rear. The tables in the bar are made from the bases of old treadle sewing machines.

Placed on the wall is a glass cabinet containing many items of horse harness and brasses, these were donated to the inn in memory of Bill Wotton, whose shire horse had worn them. Bill had been a regular at the inn, man and boy since 1914. He always sat in the same seat in the corner next to the fireplace and woe betide anyone sitting in his place; Bill reckoned that he had squatters' rights to it. It has been estimated that during his times in the inn, he had drunk over 180 000 pints. Bill sadly passed away in 1990 aged 76.

The stables, which were at the rear of the building, and were reached by going through the covered alleyway, are now used as the beer cellar. The roof of the cellar is still supported by old tree trunks forming the beams, like those originally in the main building. There is an old granite horse trough outside the cellar and water was hand pumped into it from a spring-fed well, now hidden below the alleyway.

75: Victoria Inn

North Street, Ahsburton
Tel: Ashburton (0364) 52402

The Victoria Inn is thought to date back to the 15th century although it has only been an inn for approximately a hundred years. It is known by the locals as the 'First & Last', because it is the first pub into Ashburton via North Street and the last going out. The building was once part of a series of weavers' cottages, the loft spaces of each cottage forming one long room which was used to wash and dry the fleece before being spun into yarn.

The interior of the inn appears as if time has passed it by. The main bar, which has two large fireplaces, has an assortment of old photographs connected with the inn and there are some plaques of Queen Victoria, who reigned between 1837 and 1901, after whom the inn is named. Separated from the public bar by an exposed stone wall is the restaurant.

76: Walkhampton Inn

In the Village of Walkhampton, 1.5 miles from Yelverton and 0.5 mile from the B3212. Tel: Yelverton (0822) 852706

The exact date when the Inn was built is uncertain. The first record of there being a public house here is on a census return form dated 1851, which lists a Henry Barons, Head, Married, Aged 42, Victualler. It is thought that the inn could date back to the 16th century when nearby Walkhampton church was being built, although it most probably dates from the late 17th century.

When it was first built, the inn was much smaller than it is today. It has been enlarged by the acquisition of the surrounding cottages over the years.

The lounge bar was added in 1982 with the addition of the three cottages on the left of the building, two being in front, beside the road, and one behind. Access to the inn was through a door in the front of the building leading into a passageway that separated a lounge and public bar. There was also a small bar where the toilets now are.

The car park used to be a yard, enclosed by an eight feet high wall with large wooden gates. Adjoining the yard were the stables that were in constant use with the horses of lodgers staying at the inn.

The large open-plan lounge/public bar has exposed stone walls and a low beamed ceiling. The centre section of the dividing wall between the two front cottages that now make up part of the lounge has been retained and now houses the fireplace. The wooden beams on the ceiling and the wall surrounding the fireplace support a large collection of horse harness brasswear.

In the centre of the old yard there used to be a tap supplied from a spring in a field a short distance from the village. Before the mains water supply was first introduced to Walkhampton this was the village's only source of water.

77: Warren House Inn

Beside the B3212, 8 miles from Moretonhampstead.
Tel: (0822) 88208

The Warren House Inn was built in 1845 and replaced the New Inn that stood on the opposite side of the road, and which had been demolished that same year. This meant that the inn had moved from common land in the parish of North Bovey to Duchy Land. Subsequently this meant having to pay rent. When it was first built, the Warren House Inn was called The Moreton Inn and it was not until later that century that the name was changed. The reference is to the nearby rabbit warrens, where the tin miners of the locality would keep the rabbits that provided a source of fresh meat. The inn's sign shows the tinners' emblem of three rabbits in a circle, the ears of each touching the ears of the adjacent rabbit.

Standing at 1425 feet above sea level the Warren House Inn is the second highest inn in England and it enjoys some of Dartmoor's most splendid views. The lofty peaks of Hookney Tor, Birch Tor and Hameldon Ridge look down upon it and just through the trees of the plantation to the right, Bellever Tor can be seen. There is a peat fire burning in the public bar that is reputed to have been burning for over one hundred years.

Many years ago the Inn was isolated during a snow storm, and a weary traveller called at the inn requesting accommodation. The landlord showed him to the spare room upstairs, and while the visitor unpacked his few belongings, he noticed a large wooden chest standing in the corner of the inn. After looking at it for a while he decided to look in it to see what it contained, what he saw caused him a terrible fright and he ran screaming down the stairs, shouting 'There's a body in my room, there's a body in my room.' To this the landlord replied, 'Don't worry, tiz only Feyther.' Father had died a few weeks earlier, but because of the prolonged bad weather his corpse was salted-down to await burial at the parish church.

78: Watermans Arms ─────

Chapel Street, Buckfastleigh
Tel: Buckfastleigh (0364) 43200

The Watermans Arms dates from the 16th century and was originally thought to have been a cider house. It has been suggested that the correct name of the Inn is the Waterman Arms. A previous inn sign showed the family crest of the Waterman family who many years ago appear to have had some connection with Buckfastleigh. The inn now comprises a public bar, family room and the 'Dartmoor Lounge'. The latter has a low ceiling, subdued lighting from hidden wall lights and old coach lamps, and there is a beautiful exposed-stone fireplace.

The inn is thought to be haunted by the ghost of a woman whose shadowy figure has been seen in the small room above the archway leading to the inn's car park, and which used to adjoin the hayloft (now, and since

the early 1960s, a betting shop). This ghostly figure has since been seen in a corner of the Dartmoor Lounge.

79: Welcome Stranger

On the A38 at Bickington, 1 mile from Drumbridges.
Tel: Bickington (0626) 821224

The Welcome Stranger inn was built in 1750 when the turnpike road between Chudleigh and Plymouth was being constructed, and was originally a coaching inn called the New Inn. The barn beside the inn used to be the stables.

On 26 July 1772 the landlord opened the front door and found an abandoned baby girl lying on the doorstep. As the inn lies within the parish of Ilsington, she was taken to the vicarage. There is an entry in the church records relating to the event. She was christened Mary Inn and was brought

up by one of the women of the village; her upkeep being paid for out of parish funds. She married William Coleman in the church of St Michael's, Ilsington, in 1793. She died in 1856 aged 84 years and is buried in Ilsington churchyard.

Another unusual event took place here in the 1840s, unfortunately without a happy ending. A ten-year-old girl fell out of an upstairs window and died. Her ghost comes back to haunt the inn when she can be heard crying.

In the 1950s the name of the Inn was changed to the Welcome Stranger maybe a reference to the event in 1820. The previous inn's sign used to show a stork cradling a baby, but following complaints from certain women's groups, it had to be changed to its present sign, with the crossed hands.

80: White Hart Hotel

In the Square, Moretonhampstead, 14 miles from Exeter.
Tel: Moretonhampstead (0647) 40406

The White Hart dates from the 18th century, having been built on the site of several houses that had earlier been destroyed by fire. The inn was sold to its first owner for £130. The costs of the solicitor handling the transaction was £185.8s.6d.

During the reign of George III, the White Hart became a busy post inn for the Exeter to Plymouth mail coaches which stopped here to change horses and load/unload mail for the surrounding area. This was before the coming of the railway to Moretonhampstead in 1867. The stables were situated at the rear of the building and to reach them the horses were led through the front door, along the wide passage and then down a slope to the stables. They have since been converted into a conference room.

Over the years the White Hart has been a popular meeting place. During the Napoleonic Wars, when French prisoners of war were held at Princetown, officers on parole would meet here. The Dartmoor Tinners'

Great Court, which was made up of 96 Jurates from the Stannary towns of Chagford, Ashburton, Plympton and Tavistock held their last meeting in the White Hart on 11 December 1786. There were at least thirteen meetings of this court. On 11 December 1986 an anniversary dinner was held and 96 people attended.

The public bar with its oak-beamed ceiling and large fireplace, has, hanging on the wall in a recess, a framed newspaper cutting. This informs of the tragic event which befell one of the customers who had called at the inn on the 16 July 1835, just as the fair at Moretonhampstead was coming to a close. Farmer Jonathan May aged 48 years and living at Dunsford, went into the White Hart to conclude a business deal, during which he displayed £80 in gold and notes. There were many other people in the inn at the time and his actions did not go unnoticed, especially by two strangers who showed a great deal of interest. After his final drink he mounted his horse and set out for his home five miles away. His riderless horse was later seen returning to Moretonhampstead with the saddle between its legs. The farmer was found a mile away at Jacob's Well. He had been pulled from his horse, knocked unconscious and robbed. He was then taken back to the White Hart where he died the following day. The inquest was held in what is now the dining room. Two men, Thomas Oliver (alias Buckingham Joe) and Edmund Galley (alias Dick Turpin) were arrested for the crime and they were tried at the Devon Assize in July 1836. Both men were found guilty and sentenced to death, although Thomas Oliver strenuously stated, right up to the time that he went to the gallows, that Galley was innocent. After many appeals Galley's sentence was commuted to transportation to Australia. Forty-two years later Galley sent a letter to Thomas Latimer who was the proprietor of the *Western Times* informing him that he had heard of a certain John French who had also been transported, for a different crime, stating that he had been the Dick Turpin who had helped to rob and murder farmer Jonathan May. In 1881 after a great deal of lobbying in Parliament by Thomas Latimer, Edmund Galley, who was then 80 years old was acquitted of the crime and awarded £1000 compensation.

81: White Horse Inn

In Court Street, Moretonhampstead, 14 miles from Exeter.
Tel: Moretonhampstead (0647) 40242

The White Horse dates from 1632, although it wasn't until 1793 that the first record of it being an inn appears. For just over a hundred years it was in the hands of the Gray Family 1835-1940 and was known as The Grays Hotel. For many years the inn was a busy coaching inn with a yard and stables at the rear of the building. Placed along the far side of the yard until recently, when it was converted into a restaurant, was the 'Denno Bar', very popular with the locals.

On the 11 September 1838 a fire broke-out at the White Horse which, within two hours, had destroyed fourteen nearby houses. Concern was expressed over the fact that stored in the slaughterhouse at the rear of the inn was a small barrel of gunpowder.

Firefighters had to stand clear until it had exploded before they were able to tackle the blaze. It soon became apparent though that help was needed and a messenger was despatched to Exeter on horseback. Three horse-drawn appliances arrived, the first some hours after the fire started. Samuel Gray, proprietor of the White Horse, suffered great loss with his inn burnt down along with the outbuildings.

Improved Double-Earrel Portable Fire Engine,
very powerful, compact and cheap.

82: White Thorn Inn

In the south-western corner of Dartmoor, 10 miles north-east of
Plymouth and 10 miles south-east from Tavistock. Tel: (075539) 245

The history of the present day White Thorn is relatively short, the Inn
having been built in the 1930s. It retained its original form until a few years
ago when the ground floor underwent a complete refurbishment. The walls
between the public bar and the ground floor bedroom and the lounge bar
were removed to make the large open public bar/lounge bar seen today.
There is now a restaurant upstairs.

There are no resident ghosts staying here, but there is 'Flash' the Dartmoor pony, owned by the landlord. Flash is occasionally allowed during the summer months into the public bar where he can indulge himself in a pint of beer and packet of crisps. His strange habits are well known to the locals.

The White Thorn Cottage

The previous White Thorn Inn is now White Thorn Cottage, situated a few yards away on the opposite side of the car park. This building is over 200 years old and it is rumoured that, just like the Warren House Inn, there was a peat fire burning there which hadn't been allowed to go out for almost 160 years. William Crossing states in his famous book *Guide to Dartmoor*, that he remembered seeing it in 1873 when it had not been allowed to go out for at least forty years.